**LIVERPOOL EVERYMAN AND PLAYHOUSE
IN ASSOCIATION WITH SHARED EXPERIENCE PRESENT**

TEN TINY TOES

BY ESTHER WILSON

First performed on 13 June 2008 at the Liverpool Everyman

The theatres' 2008 programme is supported by the
Liverpool Cultur
2008 European C

Liverpool Everyman and Playhouse

About the Theatres

Liverpool has an illustrious theatrical heritage, with the Everyman and Playhouse producing many of this country's most acclaimed writers, performers and theatre-makers. In January 2004 we introduced our 'Made in Liverpool' programme. We have been continually in production, creating shows which have ensured that 'Made in Liverpool' is widely recognised as a stamp of theatrical quality.

But there is more to these theatres than simply the work on our stages. We have a busy Literary Department, working to nurture the next generation of Liverpool Playwrights. A wide-ranging community department takes our work to all corners of the city and surrounding areas, and works in partnership with schools, colleges, youth and community groups to open up the theatre to all. The Everyman and Playhouse Youth Theatre trains and develops the theatrical talent of the future.

Our aim is for these theatres to be an engine for creative excellence, artistic adventure, and audience involvement; firmly rooted in our community, yet both national and international in scope and ambition.

'the thrillingly revitalised Liverpool Everyman' The Observer

13 Hope Street, Liverpool L1 9BH
Liverpool Everyman and Playhouse is a registered charity no. 1081229
www.everymanplayhouse.com

Ten Tiny Toes was commissioned with sponsorship from Lime Pictures

Funders

    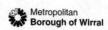

With thanks to:
Mike McCann and British Military Fitness, Simon Hodgson, Hampstead Theatre, Shared Experience, Rose Gentle

Dedicated to innovation and exploration, Shared Experience has pioneered a distinctive performance style that celebrates the union of physical and text-based theatre. Our work ranges from literary adaptations to contemporary and classic drama which has enjoyed outstanding artistic and critical acclaim at home and abroad.

Shared Experience creates theatre that goes beyond our everyday lives, giving form to the hidden world of emotion and imagination. At the heart of our work is the power and excitement of the performer's physical presence and the collaboration between actor and audience – a shared experience.

Following our successful visit in Spring 2007 with **Kindertransport**, we are very pleased to return to the Liverpool Everyman and Playhouse for this co-production of **Ten Tiny Toes**.

Touring next:

MINE
written & directed by Polly Teale
2nd October – 22nd November 2008

Most recent production:

WAR AND PEACE
'*Triumphant Theatre*' Sunday Times; '*Enthralling*' FT;
'*Magnificent*' Telegraph; '*Glorious*' Guardian; '*A Masterpiece*' Spectator;
'*Epic Achievement*' Times

From our audience:
'*The most remarkable thing I have ever seen on a stage.*'
'*This is genius. This is theatre. This is what theatre is for.*'

Shared Experience
Joint Artistic Directors Nancy Meckler & Polly Teale
admin@sharedexperience.org.uk
www.sharedexperience.org.uk

Credits

Cast (in alphabetical order)

Maya Johnson	**Joanna Bacon**
Lucy Cope	**Fionnuala Dorrity**
Michael Kent	**David Lyons**
Mike Kent/Colonel Weston	**Barry McCormick**
Gill Kent	**Lisa Parry**
Chris Kent/Reporter	**Joe Shipman**
Olivia Weston	**Paula Stockbridge**

Company

Writer	**Esther Wilson**
Director	**Polly Teale**
Designer	**Angela Simpson**
Lighting Designer	**Chris Davey**
Music and Sound Designer	**Peter Salem**
Video Designer	**Lorna Heavey**
Casting Director	**Kay Magson CDG**
Costume Supervisor	**Fi Carrington**
Assistant Director	**Chris Tomlinson**
Dialect Coach	**Jan Haydn Rowles**
Dramaturg	**Suzanne Bell**
Production Manager	**Sean Pritchard**
Stage Manager	**Linda J. Kyle**
Deputy Stage Manager	**Ella May McDermott**
Assistant Stage Manager	**Rebecca Carnell**
Lighting Operator	**Andy Webster**
Sound AV Operator	**Marc Williams**

Joanna Bacon
Maya Johnson

Joanna's theatre credits include:
Frozen (Manchester Library); *Romeo and Juliet* (Battersea Arts Centre); *Death of a Salesman* and *Saved* (Bolton Octagon Theatre); *Love and Money* (Royal Exchange/Young Vic Theatre); *Beaver Coat* (Finborough Theatre); *Cancer Tales* (Ipswich Wolsey Theatre); *House/Garden* (Salisbury Playhouse); *Iphigenia* (Sheffield Crucible Theatre); *Perfect Days* (Manchester Library Theatre); *Made of Stone* (Royal Court Theatre); *Rise and Fall of Little Voice* (Salisbury Playhouse Theatre) and *Somewhere* and *Pig's Ear* (Liverpool Playhouse).

Television credits include: *Holby City*, *Angel of Death*, *Family Man*, *Little Britain*, *Murder Prevention*, *Fifteen Storeys High*, *Second Generation*, *Wire in the Blood*, *Secret Britain: Smugglers*, *Touch of Frost*, *Chambers*, *American Freak* and *The Invisibles*.

Film credits include: *Rocknrolla*, *Venus*, *Love Actually*, *Revelations*, *Last Orders*, *The Prince and the Pauper* and *Easy Virtue*.

Fionnuala Dorrity
Lucy Cope

Fionnuala's theatre credits include: *The Ugly Duckling* (Sheffield Theatres/Nottingham Playhouse); *In Search of Fabulous Beasts* (Fuse/Unity Theatre); *Doctor Faustus* (Third Party); *Noah's Ark* (Walk the Plank); *Beauty* (Base Chorus/Unity Theatre); *Backwater* (Spike Theatre); *Out of the Blue* (Everyman Theatre, tour); *Soulskin* (Red Ladder); *The Corrupted Angel* (Base Chorus/Royal Opera House); *Happy Xmas (War Is Over)* (Spike Theatre); *Beauty and the Beast* and *No Fear* (Hope Street) and *All For Money* (Hickscorner Productions).

Cabaret includes: *The Potting Shed* (Walk the Plank).

Short film credits include: *Cappuccino* and *Boris Listens*.

Site-specific performance includes: *The Tower of the Light* (Walk the Plank) and *Halloween Lantern Carnival* (Zho/Liverpool Lantern Co.).

David Lyons
Michael Kent

David's theatre credits include:
The Good Hope, Robin Hood, Cymbeline, The Relapse, Old Time Music Hall, The Cherry Orchard and *Plasticine* (East 15 Acting School).

Television credits includes:
Stuart Gordon in *Brookside.*

Short film credits include:
Locket.

Barry McCormick
Mike Kent/Colonel Weston

Barry's theatre credits include:
Little Voice (Watermill Theatre); *Mother Courage* (English Touring Theatre); *Julius Caesar* (Hull Truck Theatre Co.); *Ma Rainey's Black Bottom* (Liverpool Playhouse); *Shang-A-Lang* (Chichester Festival Theatre); *The Sound of Fury* (Liverpool Playhouse); *Mayor of Casterbridge* and *Snowman* (Snap Theatre Company); *Duchess of Malfi* (Chelsea Centre) and *Henry VI Parts I – III* (Man in the Moon).

Television credits include: *Lillies, Love in Hyde Park, Hollyoaks, Where the Heart Is, Dream Team, The Court Room, Merseybeat, Doctors, The Bill, Brookside, In Deep, Casualty, Family Affairs, London's Burning, Comics, And the Beat Goes On* and *Bugs.*

Film credits include: *The Wolfman, Miss Potter, Mutant Chronicles, Silent Cry, Another Bobby O'Hara Story* and *MacGyver.*

Lisa Parry
Gill Kent

Lisa's rehearsed readings include: *Purple Patch* (The Works); *Everyword* and *My Eyes...Your Smile* (Liverpool Everyman).

Television credits includes: *Emmerdale* and *The Bill*.

Radio credits include: *Tin Man*, *The Wire*, *Unprotected* and *The Grove*.

This is Lisa's first production for the Everyman.

Joe Shipman
Chris Kent/Reporter

Joe's theatre credits include: *Slow Time* (20 Stories High); *The Way Home* (Liverpool Everyman); *Rush* (Liverpool Museums); *Wrong Place Right Time* (Ifaq); *Free To Do As I Say* (Fall Off the Floor); *Macbeth* (Hope Street Limited); *Rollercoaster* (Hope Street Healthy Arts); *Popcorn* (Moonlight Productions) and *The Trial* (Unity Theatre).

Radio credits include: *Big Toe Radio Show*, *Culture* and *Girl 2008*.

Short film credits include: *Unintended* and *The Bowden Tapes*.

Paula Stockbridge
Olivia Weston

Paula's theatre credits include:
A Touch of the Sun (Salisbury
Playhouse, tour); *Press Cuttings,
How He Lied to Her Husband, The
Madras House, Major Barbara, Dona
Rosita, The House of Bernarda Alba,
Hurting* and *Winner Takes All*
(Orange Tree); *Once We Were
Mothers* (New Vic, Newcastle-
under-Lyme); *Things We Do For
Love* (Frankfurt); *Private Lives* (York
Theatre Royal); *The Memory of Water*
(Vienna); *Absurd Person Singular, The
Four Alice Baker*s and *Seasons
Greetings* (Birmingham Repertory
Theatre); *Othello* and *Necklaces*
(Talawa Theatre Company); *Les
Liaisons Dangereuses* (Royal
Shakespeare Company); *Jane Eyre*
(Bill Kenwright Ltd); *The Winslow
Boy* (West Yorkshire Playhouse); *A
Midsummer Night's Dream* (English
Touring Theatre) and *Bow Down*
(National Theatre Studio).

Television credits include: *The
Bill, Silent Witness, Most Mysterious
Murders, Merseybeat, A is for Acid, The
Belfry Witches, September Song, Crime
Traveller, Capital City* and *The Saint*.

Esther Wilson
Writer

Esther was the lead writer on
Unprotected which was performed at
the Everyman before transferring to
the Edinburgh Fringe Festival
where it won an Amnesty
International Freedom of
Expression Award. A radio version
of the play was transmitted on BBC
Radio 4 and was shortlisted for a
Prix Europa award. Her 2004 radio
play *Hiding Leonard Cohen* was the
winner of Mental Health in
Media's Best Radio Drama Award.

Other writing credits include:
Hush Little Baby and *The Heroic
Pursuits of Darleen Fyles* (BBC Radio
4); *Writing of Harlots* (BBC Free
Thinking Festival); *Soulskin* (Red
Ladder Theatre Company, national
tour); *Halloween* (The Liverpool
Lantern Company/Zho);
Rollercoaster, Whirlwind, Bubblegum
and *Bling* (Hope Street); *Wounded*
and *Trapped* (Unity Theatre); *Noah's
Ark* (Walk the Plank, national tour)
and *The Swimming Man* (BBC
Northern Exposure Award for
Short Film).

Esther is currently writing *The
Quiet Little Englishman* for Zho
Theatre and an episode of Jimmy
McGovern's multi-award-winning
The Street.

Polly Teale
Director

Polly is Joint Artistic Director of Shared Experience for whom she recently co-directed *War and Peace* with Nancy Meckler (co-production with Nottingham Playhouse and Hampstead Theatre).

For Shared Experience:
Kindertransport, *Jane Eyre* (adapted and directed, tour and West End), *Brontë*, *After Mrs Rochester* (written and directed, tour and West End, Best Director, Evening Standard Awards; Best West End Production, Time Out Awards), *Madame Bovary*, *The Clearing*, *A Doll's House*, *The House of Bernarda Alba* and *Desire Under the Elms*. Co-directed with Nancy Meckler: *War and Peace* (co-production with the National Theatre) and *The Mill on the Floss*.

Other theatre includes: *Angels and Saints* (Soho Theatre); *The Glass Menagerie* (Lyceum, Edinburgh); *Miss Julie* (Young Vic); *Babies*, *Uganda* and *Catch* (Royal Court Theatre); *A Taste of Honey* (English Touring Theatre); *Somewhere* (National Theatre); *Waiting at the Water's Edge* (Bush Theatre) and *What is Seized* (Drill Hall).

Other writing includes: *Afters* (BBC Screen Two) and *Fallen* (Traverse, Edinburgh, at the Drill Hall).

Angela Simpson
Designer

Angela studied Fine Art at Middlesex University before completing the Motley Theatre Design Course.

Angela's design work includes:
War and Peace (Shared Experience/Hampstead Theatre, tour); *A Conversation* (Royal Exchange Theatre); *Darwin's Dream* (Royal Albert Hall, tour); *The Doll Tower* (LLT, Unity Theatre); *Map of the Heart* (Salisbury Playhouse); *The Pocket Dream* and *The Derby McQueen Affair* (York Theatre Royal); *The Danny Crowe Show* (Dundee Rep); *Crime and Punishment in Dalston* (Arcola Theatre); *Under the Curse* and *Habitats* (The Gate); *The Baby and Fly Pie*, *Basil and Beattie* and *Habitat* (Royal Exchange Studio); *Bread and Butter* (Southwark Playhouse); Unsung/Consuming Songs (Battersea Arts Centre); *Kom_b@* (National Theatre Studio) and *A Midsummer Night's Dream*, *Extension Treble Zero*, *Anansi* and *Boubile* (Chicken Shed Theatre Company).

Chris Davey
Lighting Designer

Chris's designs in Liverpool include: *Yellowman, The Quare Fellow, War and Peace, The Little Mermaid* and *The Odyssey*.

For the Royal Shakespeare Company: *Twelfth Night, The Winter's Tale, Pericles, Cymbeline, Alice in Wonderland, Night of the Soul, Romeo and Juliet, A Midsummer Night's Dream, Everyman, A Month in the Country, Troilus and Cressida, The Comedy of Errors, Mysteria* and *Easter*.

For the National Theatre: *Harper Reagan, The Seagull, The Pillars of the Community, A Dream Play, Iphiginia at Aulis, War and Peace* and *Baby Doll*.

Dance includes: *21* (Rambert Dance Company); *Jekyll and Hyde* (Northern Ballet Theatre) and Matthew Bourne's *The Car Man*.

Opera includes: Six seasons for GPO; *Aida* (Houston Grand Opera); *Bird of Night* (Royal Opera House); *Bluebeard* (Bregenz Festpsiele, St Polten); *Jephtha* (ENO/WNO); *The Magic Flute* (WNO); *The Rake's Progress* (Aldeburgh); and *The Picture of Dorian Gray* (Monte Carlo).

Peter Salem
Music and Sound Designer

For Shared Experience: *Orestes: Blood and Light, Brontë, A Passage to India, The Clearing, The Mill on the Floss, The House of Bernarda Alba, Jane Eyre, The Tempest, War and Peace* and *Anna Karenina*.

Other theatre credits include: *The Crucible, The Miser* and Robert Lepage's *A Midsummer Night's Dream* (National Theatre); *Julius Caesar* and *Murder in the Cathedral* (Royal Shakespeare Company) and work for the Royal Court, Traverse, Lyric Hammersmith and Nottingham Playhouse.

Film and television dramas include: *Beau Brummell, Sex, the City and Me, Falling, Trial and Retribution, Thursday the 12th, Great Expectations, Alive and Kicking, The Other Boleyn Girl, The Vice* (series 2-7) and *Painted Lady*.

Televsion documentaries include: *Francesco's Venice*, Simon Shama's *The Power of Art: Caravaggio, Thrown to the Lions, The People's Court, Sea of Cortez, 21Up-South Africa, The Spy who Caught a Cold, I Met Adolf Eichmann, Eight Hours from Paris* and *Three Salons at the Seaside*.

Lorna Heavey
Video Designer

Lorna is a multi-disciplinary artist, trained in Fine Art at Düsseldorf Art Academy (Nam June Paik and Nan Hoover) and is Artistic Director of Headfirst Foundation, a cross-platform artist's collective. Lorna was elected Fellow of Royal Society of Arts in 2004.

Video designs for theatre, dance and opera include: *Macbeth* (Broadway, Gielgud, Minerva, nominated for Olivier Award for Best Set Design, and 'Outstanding Video for a Play' Drama Desk Award for the Broadway transfer); *The Last Days of Judas Iscariot* and *Marianne Dreams* (Almeida); *The Glass Menagerie* (West End); *The Caucasian Chalk Circle* (National Theatre); *The Tempest* and *Speaking Like Magpies* (Royal Shakespeare Company, West End); *Phaedra* (Donmar Warehouse); *Vanishing Point* and *Genoa 01* (Complicité, Royal Court Theatre); *Rough Crossings*, *Faustus* and *Paradise Lost* (Headlong); *Mahabharata* (Sadler's Wells); *Dido and Aeneas* (Opera North).

Other set and video design includes: *Branded* (Old Vic Theatre); *Titus Andronicus*, *Hamlet Machine* (Battersea Arts Centre); *A Stitch in Time* and *Beautiful Beginnings* (Latchmere).

Lorna has written and directed for theatre and film.

Fi Carrington
Costume Supervisor

Fi trained in Theatre Costume Design at Mabel Fletcher Liverpool. After working at English National Opera, the Redgrave Theatre, Farnham, and the Mercury Theatre, Colchester, she began supervising shows at The Dukes Lancaster, Pitlochry Festival Theatre, Haymarket Leicester, Clwyd Theatr Cymru, Tramway Glasgow, Glasgow Repertory Company and for various touring companies.

Chris Tomlinson
Assistant Director

Chris graduated from Liverpool John Moores University in 2007. He is based in Liverpool as an actor/director.

Directing credits include: *One Step Forward One Step Back* (assistant director for DreamThinkSpeak); *The Lemon Princess* and *Iron* (Liverpool John Moores University) and *The Wiz* (Northern Academy of Performing Arts).

Theatre credits include: *The Legend of Robin Hood* (Spike Theatre); *The Bibby Line* (AS Productions); *The Brothers Grimm Fairy Tails* (MATE Edinburgh Fringe) and *Robin Hood and the Golden Arrow of Doom* (Off the Ground).

Kay Magson CDG
Casting Director

Theatre credits include: *Ma Rainey's Black Bottom, Still Life and the Astonished Heart, The Odd Couple, Dr Faustus, Who's Afraid of Virginia Woolf?, Chimps, Season's Greetings, The Tempest, The Lady of Leisure, Billy Liar* and *The Flint Street Nativity* (Liverpool Playhouse); *Brassed Off* (Liverpool Playhouse/Birmingham Repertory Theatre); *Endgame, The Electric Hills* and *Aladdin* (Liverpool Everyman); *The Solid Gold Cadillac* (Garrick Theatre); *Dangerous Corner* (West Yorkshire Playhouse/West End); *Round the Horne… Revisited, Aspects of Love, Singin' in the Rain, The Witches of Eastwick* and *All the Fun of the Fair* (national tours); and *Assassins, Amadeus* and *Shadowmouth* (Sheffield Theatres).

Kay was the resident Casting Director at West Yorkshire Playhouse for seventeen years where productions included *Beatification of Area Boy, Hamlet, Twelfth Night, The Duchess of Malfi, The Lion, the Witch and the Wardrobe, Don Quixote, Bollywood Jane, Salonika*. She is also a member of the Casting Directors' Guild of Great Britain.

Jan Haydn Rowles
Dialect Coach

Jan is a voice and dialect coach for theatre, TV and film. She is currently Head of Voice for Shakespeare's Globe Theatre's 2008 season.

Recent productions include: *Kindertransport* (Shared Experience, tour); *Betrayal* and *Absurdia* (Donmar Warehouse); *Alaska, The Pain and the Itch* and *My Child* (Royal Court Theatre); *The Merchant of Venice* and *Holding Fire!* (Shakespeare's Globe); *Henry V, The Children's House* and *Pretend You Have Big Buildings* (Manchester Royal Exchange); and *She Stoops to Conquer* (Birmingham Rep). Jan has also worked on over twenty productions for the Royal Shakespeare Company, including *Breakfast with Mugabe, The American Pilot, Twelfth Night* and *A Midsummer Night's Dream*.

Television credits include: *Faking It* (series 4), *The Football Manager* and *The Fashion Designer*.

Film credits include: *Brothers of the Head, Brick Lane* and *When Did You Last See Your Father*.

Jan is a co-author with Edda Sharpe of *How To Do Accents* (Oberon Books).

TEN TINY TOES

Esther Wilson

For my sons, Paul Ryan Wilson and Daniel Guy Wilson

*Great respect to Military Families Against the War
for their courage and determination
in the pursuit of truth and justice*

*Thank you to all the mothers who opened their hearts to me;
thank you to Polly Teale at Shared Experience; and finally,
thank you to Suzanne Bell who helped make this project
possible.*

Characters

The Mothers
GILL KENT, *early forties*
LUCY COPE, *early forties*
OLIVIA WESTON, *late forties*
MAYA JOHNSON, *fifties*

The Fathers
MIKE KENT, *late forties – fifties*
COLONEL WESTON, *late forties – fifties*

The Sons
MICHAEL KENT, *twenty-three*
CHRIS KENT, *nineteen*

POLICEMAN

This play is based on extensive interviews with mothers and wives of soldiers either currently serving, or who have lost their lives, in the conflict in Iraq and Afghanistan. It is also based on time spent with Military Families Against the War, culminating in the three-day peace camp in Manchester in 2006.

A forward slash (/) in the text indicates the point at which the next speaker interrupts.

This text went to press before the end of rehearsals and so may differ slightly from the play as performed.

ACT ONE

Overture

On film, we see a montage of the following:

John Simpson running into Afghanistan with the British troops in elated mood.

The Twin Towers.

George W. Bush's 'With Us or Against Us' speech.

Tony Blair making the case for war.

Troops entering Iraq. The idea of a precise and contained military campaign.

Toppling of the Saddam Hussein statue.

News footage on the search for WMD. None found.

Images of shoot-outs, car bombs, suicide bombers, etc.

Sense of chaos.

The 7/7 carnage in London.

Things getting worse as we arrive at the present day.

Footage of a baby, just born. Still covered in blood and membrane. The baby's first cry. The baby put into its mother's arms. A primal image which could be in Iraq, England, or anywhere in the world.

Scene One

The Kent's house. Some naff daytime telly programme plays in the background. CHRIS *is trying on* MICHAEL's *uniform jacket.*

MICHAEL. You're not big enough for it, lad, get it off.

CHRIS. Oh, you reckon, do ya? (*Taking off the jacket.*) So go on. Spill.

MICHAEL. Is what it is, innit?

CHRIS. Don't be goin' all Tommy Dunn on us... (*Imitating a toothless old bloke.*) 'The Japs are a very cruel race. But it's not somethin' I wanna talk about...'

MICHAEL. It's the fucking Yanks you've gotta dodge. Tellin' ya, most of 'em are grunts. Even the officers. Think they're in a fuckin' video game. Nutters.

CHRIS. Ever get to blow somebody away?

MICHAEL. Fuck off, Christof.

CHRIS. You have, haven't ya?

MICHAEL. Behave, ya knob.

CHRIS. How close was ya?

MICHAEL. I've not come home to talk about all that.

CHRIS. I can't imagine you... Fuckin' well weird thought, that, la.

MICHAEL. Then get it outta ya head.

CHRIS. Is it harsh, like?

MICHAEL. It is what it is. End of.

CHRIS. Some of them video's on YouTube, fuckin' well sick. People gettin' wiped to Bruce fuckin' Springsteen.

MICHAEL. What have you been fillin' ya head with all that nonsense for?

CHRIS. Wanted to get a sense of… you know… what it's like out there, what you were going through, an' that. (*Beat.*) Hey? Should see me ma, 'surfing the net' now.

MICHAEL. Go 'way! Me mother? She freaked out when the Asda brought them self-serving machines in. (*Imitating.*) 'I'll go the Tesco if they're gonna make us use one of them.'

CHRIS. No word of a lie. She's even onto the bloggin' thing… MySpace… talking to people all over shop.

MICHAEL. 'Kin 'ell.

CHRIS. I'm telling ya. She said, 'I've got to get more with it. I wanna know what it's like out there for our Michael.' She goes on all these different sites, checking stuff out. (*Beat.*) First thing she does of a morning is have a look at the temperature in Basra. We're as miserable as sin cause it's pissin' it down here, and she comes in and goes, (*Imitating.*) 'A hundred. And twelve. Degrees. Our Michael must be boiling over there. I just hope he's using a high-factor sunscreen. You know how easily he burns?' Me and me dad are like… (*He shakes his head and laughs.*)

MICHAEL (*laughing*). Showing her how to use her new mobile was bad enough.

CHRIS. Bill fuckin' Gates round here now, telling ya! (*Beat.*) Thought about you every day, you know. Not a day went by… Sound like me fuckin' ma now, don't I?

MICHAEL *wrestles with him.*

MICHAEL. Turning queer? Been worryin' over me, have ya, lad? Been cryin'? / Eh?

CHRIS. Fuck off –

MICHAEL (*a girly voice*). 'I hope our Mikie is alright over there –'

CHRIS. Wasn't arsed about you, lad, looking out for a window of opportunity, isn't it? All that designer gear is mine if you get blown away. An' I'm havin' that guitar.

The wrestling turns into a half-hearted hug.

Now who's the big queer? Behave.

CHRIS *grabs* MICHAEL*'s hand.*

Jesus. What have you done to your hand?

He looks at the other one.

The state of them!

MICHAEL. It's nothin'.

CHRIS. You are joking. What've you been doing?

MICHAEL. Just need a bit of cream on them, they'll be alright in a few days. It's the breeze block, innit?

CHRIS. The breeze block?

MICHAEL (*looking through his kitbag*). For stacking in front of the tents.

CHRIS. What do you mean?

MICHAEL. Protection. The shellin' an' all that.

CHRIS. Fuckin' hell. You gotta do all that yourself, like?

MICHAEL. No. We get the officers to do it for us while we all go for a game of footie and a bevvie.

CHRIS. Shit.

MICHAEL. Don't worry. I'm good at watching me back.

CHRIS. Well, keep on being good at it. (*Beat.*) The aul fella said to me, 'Anything happens to our Mikie, we're on the first plane to Iraq an' there'll be a few dead towel-heads knocking about.'

MICHAEL. Well, nothing did happen an' I'm here now, aren't I? So? (*Beat.*) What's been happenin'? Any news? Seen anybody?

CHRIS. Same old, innit? (*Beat.*) Bumped into Sarah, couple of weeks ago.

MICHAEL. Yeah?

CHRIS. Didn't know whether to say anythin' or not, you know?

MICHAEL. All the same to me, innit? Not arsed, am I?

CHRIS. No, yeah, I know, I was just… just saying, like.

Beat.

MICHAEL. Did you talk to her?

CHRIS. Said hello, an' that.

MICHAEL. An' what?

CHRIS. Nothin'. Just chit-chat, the usual, you know?

MICHAEL. Where was this?

CHRIS. Mojo Bar.

MICHAEL. She hates it in there. 'Full of students and arty-farty wankers.'

CHRIS. It's alright. Good vibe now an' again.

Beat.

MICHAEL. Who was she with?

CHRIS. Errr… dunno. There was loads of them out.

Beat.

MICHAEL. Did she ask about me?

CHRIS. Yeah… yeah, she did.

MICHAEL. And?

CHRIS. And what? Just said you were doing great. Looking forward to coming home, an' that.

MICHAEL. And that was it?

CHRIS. More or less, yeah.

MICHAEL. 'More or less'?

CHRIS. 'Kin 'ell. That's why I wasn't sure about sayin' anythin'. I was bevvied. She was bevvied. I can't remember exactly word for word. She asked about me ma and me dad. Asked me what I was doing. I asked about their Anthony an' his football and what she was up to –

MICHAEL. Fuck me, Chris. If there's something I should know then tell me.

CHRIS. There isn't anything, alright. (*Beat*.) I'm tellin' it like I saw it. End of. Okay?

GILL *and* MIKE *enter, carrying bags of shopping.*

MIKE. Bloody hell, he's here already. The wanderer returns.

Lots of whooping and hollering as GILL *hugs* MICHAEL *and weeps. He picks her off the floor in a giant bear hug. Hugs his dad.*

MICHAEL. Alright, Dad.

GILL. Let me look at you. God, look at his tan. You look like one of them! Doesn't he look like one of them, Mike?

MIKE. That'll be the sun. What are you doing here?

MICHAEL. Want me to go back, do ya? –

GILL. Don't be soft –

MIKE. I thought you were getting the twelve o'clock from Euston?

GILL. We were gonna have it all done nice for ya. I've got a leg of lamb here. I wanted it all done special for when you got home. I even made a big welcome-home sign for out the front, an' that.

MICHAEL (*sharply*). Don't be putting up banners, Mum! Jesus. Wanna be able to show me face in the pub, don't I? (*Beat*.) I got a lift off Snowy, he's driving down to Wales to see his bird, so…

A slight moment of tension between them. Beat.

GILL. Give us another hug. I can't believe you're actually here. (*Beat*.) You look… ah, I love you. / I prayed every day, every single day.

MICHAEL. I love you too, Mum.

CHRIS (*looking through the shopping bags*). Did you get any ale, Dad?

MIKE. What do you think, soft lad?

GILL. Don't touch that wine. That's for the meal.

CHRIS (*holding up a bottle of fizz*). That's not wine, it's that fizzy shite.

CHRIS gets four cans of ale out of the bag.

GILL. Hey you! I don't mean that one, you can open that. I bought that for this exact moment. To toast our Michael, home all safe and sound. And looking bloody gorgeous. (*Another kiss.*) Chris, don't take everything out in here. Leave it, I'll sort them out.

She carries the bags through.

MICHAEL (*re: the fizz*). I fuckin' hate that stuff.

MIKE. Just have a glass to please her, we can wash it down with this.

He throws the lads a can each.

GILL (*shouting through*). And it's not 'shite' as you call it, Christopher, that was nearly eighteen quid, that. It's the proper stuff.

CHRIS (*shouting*). You trying to go all upmarket on us? (*To MICHAEL and his dad.*) Thinks she's somebody now, with the champagne.

GILL comes back in with glasses.

GILL. Laugh all you want, soft lad, but you wouldn't get that in The Railway.

In a moment of utter joy, CHRIS throws his mum over his shoulder.

CHRIS. Is it, yeah? Gonna make us all giddy, is it, Ma? All light-headed, like this?

He spins her round and round. Everyone laughs at GILL's mock protests.

GILL. Stop it, you swine, you. Tell him, Mike. Chris, put me down, you daft sod. Will you stop it! I'll swing for you, Chris. I'm warning you. I'm not messing. Mike? Tell him.

CHRIS *puts her down. She's a little unsteady on her feet. She feigns anger.*

I could have gone flying then, you soft bugger. Anything could have happened then.

CHRIS (*hugging her*). As if I'd ever let you fall.

She smacks him away, and sits down.

GILL. Honest to God, you can be one annoying little get when you want to, Christopher.

He tries tickling her, she knocks him away.

MIKE. So, how are you doing, mate?

MICHAEL. Alright, Dad. I'm okay. How've you been keeping?

MIKE. Better for havin' you here.

MIKE *gives* MICHAEL *a rough hug.*

MICHAEL. Getting a bit of a beer gut on ya there, aren't ya, Dad?

CHRIS. Six months gone, isn't he?

MIKE. I've not been out on me bike as much lately. Need to put a bit of work in, don't I?

CHRIS. Needs to lay off the ale, more like.

GILL. Does anybody want a glass of this champagne or what?

MIKE. Should stick it in the freezer for a bit first, get it nice an' cold. Wanna be havin' it at its best, don't we? At eighteen quid a pop, like.

GILL. Okay.

MIKE *takes the fizz into the kitchen.* GILL *gives* CHRIS *daggers.*

CHRIS. Well, he does.

MICHAEL. What's goin' on?

GILL. Nothing.

CHRIS. He's been knockin' it back a bit.

MICHAEL. Me dad!

GILL. He's been a bit off lately, that's all. (*Beat*.) They've had to close the workshop down. They're selling the premises.

MICHAEL. When did this happen? Why didn't somebody say somethin'?

GILL. Last month. He didn't want to worry you.

MICHAEL. That's stupid. He should have said something.

GILL. I know, I know. That's what I said, but… he said, 'Our Mikie's got more important things to be worrying about, over there.'

MICHAEL. All the same, I still need to know what's going on back home, don't I –

GILL. He insisted, Michael. Anyway. How are things with you? You don't know what to believe on the news, do you? Looks terrible.

MICHAEL. They exaggerate. (*Beat*.) And you know me, Mum. (*Putting his arm around her*.) I've sorted myself a nice cushy little number, where I know what's what and I can bide me time. (*Beat*.) It's me 'short-term savings plan'. Tellin' ya, one more tour and I'll be brewstered.

MIKE *comes back in*.

GILL. Well, we're all really proud of you, love.

CHRIS. Is right.

MICHAEL (*to* MIKE). I'm sorry about the workshop, mate, me mum's just told me.

MIKE. Yeah, I know, son. Sad, isn't it? It's been coming a while. Nobody's interested in hand-crafted furniture any more. It's the Ikea generation, isn't it? Same-day, flat-pack, cheap, stick-it-together and Bob's your uncle. We'd been gettin' more into furniture restoration anyway, you know, trying to be a bit creative with it, ride through the storm, but… If it breaks, chuck it out and get a new one, isn't it?

MICHAEL. What about Tony?

MIKE. He's the same. Gutted, but… they've had an offer on the premises from that new wine-bar chain… What are they called?

CHRIS. Mojo's. (*He glances over at* MICHAEL.)

MIKE. That's them. (*Beat.*) Tony thought they might have something for us, on the refurbishment side, like, but… they have their own way of doings things, them big firms, don't they? All kitted out the same, aren't they? (*Beat.*) Anyway, never mind all that. You've only just got home.

MICHAEL. Are you gonna be okay for money, though?

MIKE. Don't be soft, things aren't that bad, we'll be alright.

GILL. He keeps saying that, but once we've paid the mortgage off there'll be less than seven or eight grand to –

MIKE. Will you give over worrying? I've told you, something will turn up.

MICHAEL. Well, the offer's there. I've got a few bob put away to tide you over if… you know –

MICHAEL *gives his dad a reassuring pat on the back, then goes to his bag.*

GILL. Chris, take your time with that can. You're gonna be half-cut by the time we come to eat.

CHRIS. What?

MICHAEL. There's not much to spend it on out there, but… I did manage to bring a few things back for youse.

MICHAEL *takes out Arabic artefacts from his bag. A beautiful wooden box, a tablecloth, a cushion cover and a small hookah pipe.*

MIKE. Bloody hell, Gill, look at this. (*The hookah.*) I'll have to take this down The Railway, Friday night. Let young Jono and the lads use it for their wacky-baccy! Here are. (*He has a pull on it, fools around with it.*)

CHRIS (*to* MICHAEL). I can just see him down the benches with all the bag-heads, can't you?

MICHAEL. Ya daft get, that's for our Chris. / This is for you, Dad. (*The box.*) And this. (*The cushion cover.*)

GILL. You won't be smoking any of that, not in this house.

MICHAEL. It's ornamental, Mother.

MIKE. A bloody cushion cover?

The lads laugh.

I'd rather have the drugs paraphernalia!

GILL. Mike!

MICHAEL. It's for that chair you made for the conservatory, ya ungrateful auld get.

MIKE. I'm 'twistin' ya melon, man'. (*He picks up the box.*) Look at this. It's… it's beautiful this, kid. Aye, yeah. Some work gone into that, no danger. (*He's really taken with it.*) Jesus. Look at that. All hand-carved, that is. Look how fiddly all this is, Gill. (*They study it together.*)

MICHAEL. Dad, you wanna see some of the furniture they make. You'd be in your element. Chairs, tables, cabinets, an' that, all finely detailed, very ornate. Kids, as young as thirteen, fourteen, carving the most beautiful… You just come across them in some little tiny village, in some falling-down building, honest to God. And there they are, working away, making stuff like that. (*Beat.*) It's mad.

GILL (*looking at the box*). How much would you pay for that in the shops here, eh?

MICHAEL. That's what I'm saying. You can pick 'em up for next to nothin' over there. Telling ya. If you had a wad you could buy a load of stuff, bring it over here and make a fortune on it. They do appreciate good stuff. They've got an eye for it. You don't get stuff like that here, do you?

MIKE. Pure craftsmanship, that is. Definitely. Rarely see anythin' like that nowadays.

CHRIS (*gives MICHAEL the evil eye for being insensitive*). They wanna stick to making furniture, instead of bombing the crap out of our lads, who are only tryin' to help them, then, don't they?

MICHAEL. Shurrup, Chris.

CHRIS. I'm just sayin' –

GILL. Well, thanks very much for these, love. We're made up with them, aren't we, Mike?

MIKE. Yeah. Thanks, mate.

MIKE *kisses his son on the cheek.*

GILL. I'd better stick that lamb in the oven.

She touches MICHAEL*'s face and leaves.* MIKE *lowers his voice.*

MIKE (*to* CHRIS). Have you said anything to him about…

CHRIS. Alright, alright –

MICHAEL. About what?

CHRIS. I was gonna tell you later, but… (*Gives his dad daggers.*) Know what I was saying about joinin' up?

MICHAEL *groans.*

MICHAEL. You're not still… Tell me you are not serious.

MIKE. Oh, he's serious alright.

MICHAEL. You arsewipe.

CHRIS. It's what I want, Mikie. The time's right for me to do somethin' with me life.

MICHAEL. The 'time' is right? No. The time is shit. You'll do a tour right away, tellin' ya. Iraq, Afghanistan. They're getting' desperate. The TA's are up to the max. They'll be sending fuckin' traffic wardens next. (*Beat.*) Not being funny, but… I can't see you there, Chris. Just can't, mate.

CHRIS. Sayin' I couldn't handle it?

Beat.

MICHAEL. Take it you've not said anything to me ma?

MIKE. It'll be like bloody Basra round here, once she gets wind.

CHRIS. I'm over eighteen an' I know what I'm doin'. I'm sick of standing outside Cricket watching all them arl arses with more money than sense, looking down their noses at me.

MIKE. It's a job, isn't it? Pay's not bad. And you should see the Armani suit they've given him to wear. Worth a fortune. They're very upmarket, not like an ordinary shop. Loads of celebrities go there. Wayne Rooney was in there last week, with that Coleen one, wasn't he? Soft get didn't even get his autograph, like –

CHRIS *and* MICHAEL. Sod off. Wayne Rooney? Behave, Dad.

MIKE. Could have sold it on eBay, though, couldn't he? Perks of the job, innit?

CHRIS. I'm not even a fuckin' store detective, Dad. I'm a door-boy, in a suit. It's a shit job and that's all it'll ever be. That's it for me, there. Standing in a doorway watching shoppers… shop! Buying things I could never afford. Eight hours a day, bored out of me skull, opening and closing the door like a fucking tit. It's one step up from them no-marks walking up and down all day, holding a friggin' placard. See any of me mates coming and I'm like that – (*Turns his back, hiding. Beat.*) I'm sick of wasting me time. It's shit.

MICHAEL. No. I'll tell you what's shit. Your timing.

MIKE. Has there ever been any tellin' him?

CHRIS. Thinking about joining your lot, actually.

MICHAEL. Jesus –

CHRIS. Get a trade, be a mechanic, an' that. Fixin' the tanks or somethin'.

MICHAEL. 'Fixin' the tanks or somethin''! You haven't got a Scooby, have ya?

CHRIS. You *do* think I couldn't hack it, don't ya? (*Beat.*) Go on. Be honest.

MICHAEL. I think… You've not thought this through properly, mate.

CHRIS. Is it, yeah? I've thought it through loads, 'mate'. Fuckin' loads. Been on the websites, read up about it, talked to a few people –

MICHAEL. Sucked in by the adverts, was ya?

MIKE. Keep your voice down!

CHRIS. I'm not stupid. And it's my life. (*Beat*.) I've done me two days down at the ADSC. (*Army Development and Selective Committee.*) Passed me aptitude, me literacy, me medical and me physical –

MICHAEL. Who wouldn't, nowadays!

CHRIS. Passed with flying colours, actually. One of the highest scores in the group, for me physical.

MICHAEL. You'd have to be a twenty-three-stone, blind retard to fail them now!

CHRIS (*to* MIKE). See? I'm as good as him and he doesn't like it. I knew it!

MICHAEL. Behave! Things are different than when I joined up. It's not all it's cracked up to be, I'm telling you, Chris.

Beat.

CHRIS. You've not done too bad by it, though, have you? You've travelled around a bit, got a brand-new set of wheels on order. Why can't I have some of that, eh? Don't I deserve it or somethin'?

Beat.

MICHAEL. Like you say, it's your life, Chris. Do what you want.

MIKE. I don't wanna be around when your mother finds out.

CHRIS. Don't be making me feel guilty. You know what she's like.

MIKE. I know, son, it's just with all that's goin' on out there at the minute –

CHRIS. No. I'm not havin' that. She's always been the same, you know it. She'd have us locked in the house 24/7 if she could, just looking out the window, waving at the world goin' by.

Both lads know the truth of that.

MIKE. Okay. Okay.

Beat.

CHRIS. She came round when you told her you was joining up.

MICHAEL. We weren't in Iraq or Afghanistan then and I'd talked about nothin' else since I was about seven.

CHRIS. Me mind's made up. Whatever youse say. (*Beat.*) Be nice to have somebody on me side, like. Trying to make a proper career for myself, here. Youse have been goin' on at me for years to stop pissin' about. When I do. You moan.

MIKE *and* MICHAEL *look at each other.*

MICHAEL. Fuck it. If you're determined to act like a tube I might as well make a bit of dough outta ya.

CHRIS. What do you mean?

MICHAEL. Persuading some plank to join up and get 'em through the basics should make me about… £1300.

CHRIS. Serious?

MICHAEL. Yep. Recruitment drive, innit? 'Cause, oddly enough, we're overworked yet bizarrely understaffed. Soft lad.

He offers CHRIS *his hand. Beat.*

CHRIS. Get in. Fifty-fifty.

MICHAEL. Sixty-forty –

MIKE. Jesus. That's blood money, that.

CHRIS. Yeah, an' it's my fuckin' blood, so it's fifty-fifty or no deal.

Laughing, they shake on it.

MIKE. Not everything's a joke, you know, some things are serious. You want to think about other people, the pair of youse.

MICHAEL. We're only messing, Dad, come on –

CHRIS. It was a joke.

GILL (*offstage*). Mike? Can you come and sharpen this carving knife for us? This wouldn't cut through butter.

MIKE *leaves*.

MICHAEL. You're about to do the deed, aren't ya?

CHRIS. Yeah. Going in tomorrow. (*Beat.*) No going back, then.

MICHAEL. Thought as much.

CHRIS. Told you. I made me mind up.

Beat.

MICHAEL. How's the old man been, since the shop, an' that?

CHRIS. Worse than her. Tellin' ya. He's turning into an old woman.

MICHAEL. That's not stopping ya, though, is it?

CHRIS. Don't be giving me any fuckin' guilt-trip shite. I'm not having it –

MICHAEL. Okay. Sorry. (*Beat.*) I worry about you, though, lad.

CHRIS. You've gotta give me some credit, Mikie.

Beat.

MICHAEL. Remember when we went to Robin Hood's Bay with the Colemans? And you and Alex went off on your own and me and Susan were looking for youse for ages?

CHRIS. I fuckin' hated that Susan Coleman.

MICHAEL. She kept winding me up, saying there were sinky sands round there and you and Alex would probably be stuck up to your waist, an' that.

CHRIS. She was always buzzing off ya. Fat bitch.

MICHAEL. No… What I mean is… That's when I realised…

CHRIS. You don't have to say anythin', Mikie. (*Beat.*) Alex used to watch her having a shower. He reckoned you and her were messing about on that holiday. Did you get a grip of her, then? Did ya?

MICHAEL. Just shut up a minute. Out there… it's… well… You're gonna have to make choices, Chris. Trust me.

CHRIS. I'm not soft, Mikie. I can look after myself. If I get to go, I'll go. I'm not scared.

MICHAEL. Whatever they tell you in your training… there'll be difficult… moral… decisions –

CHRIS. What are you on about?

MICHAEL. Just keep your head down, watch yourself and look out for your mates. Everything else is bullshit.

CHRIS. Well, obviously, if I end up going.

MIKE and GILL enter with the fizz. She gives the bottle to MICHAEL.

GILL. Go on, love, it's your day. You open it.

MICHAEL *pops the cork.* GILL *starts pouring the fizz.*

MIKE. Welcome home, lad. Here's to you.

GILL *and* CHRIS. To Michael. / Our Mikie.

MICHAEL. And to our Chris.

The men are uncomfortable.

GILL. What? (*Beat.*) What is it?

A TV advert for the army is shown on a screen. Images include soldiers running through a jungle, wading through water, shooting on exercise, skiing down a mountain, working together in unison and parachuting out of a plane.

VOICE-OVER. For the teamwork, for the training, for the challenge. Against enemies, against the elements, against the odds. For the travel, the action, for adventure. With stealth, with precision, with pride. As a unit, as a team, through it all, together. Light Role Infantry. Forward as one.

Scene Two

Westminster Square. MAYA JOHNSON reads the names of the soldiers killed in the Iraq War. Each name is celebrated with the ringing of a bell. The other three MOTHERS are wrapping various basic equipment up, to send to their sons. Army boots, jackets, creams, lotions, bottled water and basic first-aid equipment. Pouring whiskey into shampoo bottles. As MAYA reads, a POLICEMAN approaches her and tries to interrupt. She ignores him.

MAYA. Sergeant Joseph Johnson, thirty-three.

Bell.

Captain Philip Guy, twenty-nine.

Bell.

Naval Rating Ian Seymour.

Bell.

Warrant Officer Second Class Mark Stratford.

Bell.

POLICEMAN. You've been warned three times today. If you don't move on and stop causing a disturbance, I'm going to have to arrest you.

MAYA *gets louder as the* POLICEMAN *gets more desperate.*

MAYA. Marine Sholto 'Sonic' Hedenskog, twenty-five.

Bell.

POLICEMAN. I've tried explaining the situation to you, I've been very reasonable, but you seem insistent on ruining my shift.

He tries to lead her away, but she continues. He's aware of the potentially embarrassing situation.

MAYA. Lance Bombardier Llywelyn 'Welly' Evans, twenty-four.

Bell.

Colour Sergeant John Cecil, thirty-six.

Bell.

Major Jason Ward, thirty-four.

Bell.

POLICEMAN. I don't need the paperwork and you don't need the hassle. Are you going to move or not?

MAYA. Sergeant Les Hehir, thirty-four.

Bell.

Lieutenant Philip Green, thirty-one.

Bell.

Lieutenant Tony King, thirty-five.

Bell.

POLICEMAN. You're taking the piss now.

MAYA. Lieutenant James Williams, twenty-eight.

Bell.

Lieutenant Philip West, thirty-two.

Bell.

Lieutenant Marc Lawrence, mid-twenties.

Bell.

Lieutenant Andrew Wilson, thirty-six.

POLICEMAN (*into his radio*). Control? Can I have assistance to this location? Charlie Whiskey. [Westminster Square.] (*Beat.*) Yeah, a van. For one person – over.

MRS WESTON *and* LUCY COPE *step forward.*

MRS WESTON. Your son needs your support.

LUCY. My son has my support.

MRS WESTON. No British soldier could possibly endorse this campaign, you do understand that, don't you?

LUCY. That's between him and me.

MRS WESTON. Mrs Cope. (*Beat.*) The men under my husband's command will see this as an act of disloyalty. Reading stories about families speaking out against them –

LUCY. We're not against the soldiers in the regiment.

MRS WESTON. Speak out against the army and you speak out against the men –

LUCY. We're speaking out on *behalf* of them. (*Beat.*) They've sent you along to try a little emotional blackmail, haven't they? 'Woman to woman.'

MRS WESTON. No one sent me. I came because I believe that you're doing more harm than good by seeking out publicity like this. It's a misguided… The men want to be allowed to get on with their jobs. That's all they want, Mrs Cope. Really.

LUCY. I disagree. They're fed up with having to make do and mend. With the terrible conditions they're having to put up with. They haven't got the proper equipment. They're getting mortared on a daily basis and they're sleeping in tents. They're getting killed in their sleep. Not the officers… just the NCOs. But they aren't in a position to complain. Don't you see anything wrong in that?

MRS WESTON. Mrs Cope, can we take the emotion out of this, please?

LUCY. Oddly enough, no, I can't. Why, can you?

Beat.

MRS WESTON. Men aren't press-ganged into joining the forces. They do so because they choose to and they take all that that entails. Your son is a grown man who entered into a contract. You should be proud –

LUCY. There was no one more proud when I saw my son in his uniform for the first time. There are photographs all over the hall. But the things they have to put up with, lack of basic provisions… It's wrong. (*Beat.*) Wouldn't you agree?

MRS WESTON. It is a difficult and complex situation but they are trained to deal with adversity. It's their duty. (*Beat*.) I think you're being manipulated.

LUCY. You haven't answered my question –

MRS WESTON. By unscrupulous people with a political agenda.

LUCY. What do you mean?

MRS WESTON. These… left-wing agitators –

LUCY *laughs*.

– these people don't really have your son's interest at heart. (*Beat*.) You must see that you're making things difficult for him? For the entire regiment?

LUCY. He gets shot at every day, how much more difficult can things get? I can't just sit back and wait… I just can't. (*Beat*.) And you still haven't answered –

MRS WESTON. Has there ever been a war without casualties?

LUCY. Mrs Weston, can we take the emotion out of this, please?

Beat.

MRS WESTON. I won't waste any more of your time, Mrs Cope. (*She goes to leave*.)

LUCY. What about the Weapons of Mass Destruction?

Beat.

MRS WESTON. We have to deal with the situation as it is now. We can't just cut and run. We have a moral obligation to help the Iraqis rebuild –

LUCY. We wouldn't need to help them rebuild if we hadn't razed the place to the ground in the first place. Do you or do you not think that was wrong?

MRS WESTON. What about the gassing of those Kurds we've read about, in the press? The mass graves they found? The years of oppression, suffering? His own people testified to that. He arrested, tortured and killed people, whoever he considered to be a traitor. (*Beat*.) Whatever you say, Mrs Cope, I am proud that our country helped to bring about –

LUCY. Nothing to do with the oil, then? Or the contracts to do all that rebuilding? (*Beat*.) You needed to talk to me, didn't you? You're struggling with it all yourself, aren't you? That's why you came to see me.

MRS WESTON. I came on behalf of my husband. And as a mother. (*Beat*.) My son is a serving officer in Afghanistan. It's my duty to support him. I'm proud of him. I don't want anything to jeopardise his position. (*Beat*.) I… I believe that we can best help our sons by sticking together, Mrs Cope. (*Beat*.) That's the only reason I came.

LUCY. My son wanted to be a car mechanic. From when he first started school. We've lived in Walthamstow fourteen years, but lately, round here, things have been getting worse. There are them other type of 'soldiers' that the papers are going on about, now. Angry kids, riding around on bikes, with guns, fighting, shooting at each other. He didn't want to get mixed up with all that. He wanted to be a car mechanic, that's all. Never mentioned joining the army. (*Beat*.) They recruited him from outside the dole. Picked him up in a big fancy car, introduced him to lads the same age, designer gear, cars, money in their pockets. (*Beat*.) He's six-foot-three, our Greg… never been in any trouble. We always knew where he was. (*Beat*.) The army told him he could get a trade. Learn about cars. 'Best training in the country. Do a couple of years, save a bit, come out and who knows?' (*Beat*.) If our Greg had been an apprentice mechanic he'd have had to train for three years before he'd have been let loose on a car. Three years. (*Beat*.) Twenty-four weeks and they stick a gun in his hand and send him to a war zone. How can that be right, Mrs Weston? (*Beat*.) He never even knew where Iraq was. (*Beat*.) We thought it was all done and dusted… just a matter of 'clearing up'. 'The battle for hearts and minds.' Ha. He'd been there a week when he rang me. 'We're not peacekeepers, Mum. The Iraqis hate us, they don't want us here.' (*Beat*.) He won't speak to me on the phone any more. He knows it upsets me and he's trying to be a man. He's trying to protect me. Lads like mine are ten a penny, aren't they? 'Cannon fodder,' as my granddad used to say. (*Beat.*) I've got to speak out. It's my only option. See, your son's never going to be thought of in those terms, is he, Mrs Weston? Your son's never going to be in any real danger. It's easy for you. You don't have to lose too much sleep over your son. (*Beat.*) He'll be barking out orders somewhere right at the back, safe and sound.

MRS WESTON *slaps* LUCY *across the face. The house is 'rocked' by an explosion. A grainy image of soldiers in a shoot-out. White noise signifies the shutting down of satellite communications. Andrew's death?* MRS WESTON *is more upset about the slap than* LUCY *is.*

MRS WESTON. I'm… I'm sorry. Really. I should never… I'm sorry. (*She goes to leave.*) I want you to know that my son, Andrew, is a fine officer, Mrs Cope. There isn't anything he would expect his men to do that he wouldn't do himself. I can assure you of that. (*She leaves.*)

MAYA *continues with her roll-call.*

MAYA. Captain David Jones, twenty-nine.

Bell.

POLICEMAN. Maya Johnson, I'm arresting you for causing a disturbance and for breaching the peace. You have the right to remain silent, but anything you do say –

She gets louder as the POLICEMAN *leads her off.*

MAYA. Trooper David Jeffrey Clarke, nineteen.

Bell.

Private Andrew Kelly, eighteen.

Bell.

Private Ryan Thomas, eighteen.

Bell.

Private Lee O'Callaghan, twenty.

Bell.

The sound of a guitar.

Scene Three

The MOTHERS *come forward. They are in their own homes.*
GILL *is with* CHRIS, *she's putting* MIKE's *cushion cover on.*
LUCY *is texting on her mobile.* MRS WESTON *looks through
her son's things. A hat, a belt, some photographs, a flag and a
letter. It's the elephant in the room for her.* MICHAEL *strums
his guitar, watches the scene. He's in a world of his own, dis-
tracted, building to something bad.*

GILL. One can't wait to come home and one can't wait to get
away. Funny old world, isn't it?

> CHRIS *watches her struggle with trying to fit the cushion
> into the cover.*

CHRIS. I wanna do something… worthwhile.

GILL. So you say.

CHRIS. I'm not a kid any more, Mum. I'm sorry.

GILL. It's your life, no need to apologise.

CHRIS. Then why can't you be happy for me?

GILL. Why would I be happy at the prospect of months and
months sat here biting me nails, worrying? I can't stop you
going, Christopher, but I don't have to be over the moon
about it.

> *Beat.*

CHRIS. What is there, for me, round here? Eh? You tell me.

GILL. You've not had that job that long. I thought you liked it
there. (*Beat.*) Till something better came along.

CHRIS. Nothing better is gonna come along. Look at me dad.
What's he gonna do now? Retrain again, like he did when he
was laid off from the docks? He's right, Mum. People don't
wanna make things any more, they wanna buy things. That's
why there's loads of shit going down all the time. You need
money to buy things. And people like me have got no chance
of making any. Not legit anyway. (*Beat.*) I'm sick of walking

six paces behind, ya get me? Living for the weekends.
(*Beat.*) That's no life, is it? It's doin' me head in, Mum.

GILL. Why didn't you talk to me about it first, Chris?

CHRIS. You'd have only tried to stop me. I've gotta make me
own decisions. (*Beat.*) I can't help how I feel.

MICHAEL's *strumming gets more frantic.*

GILL (*fighting back tears*). Trouble is… neither can I.

CHRIS *leaves and stands, watching her.* GILL *moves
towards the TV. She holds the cushion cover almost like she's
holding a baby.* MICHAEL *stops strumming and watches. A
moment of silence before an over-loud dialling tone, the
beep-beep of a computer trying to connect to the internet and
a million text-message sounds invade the space. Everyone
reacts then silence.* LUCY *steps forward.*

LUCY (*on the phone*). Have you heard anything? Anything at
all? (*Beat.*) Oh Christ. (*Beat.*) Everything will be shut down
for twenty-four hours, now. MSN, e-mail, phones, satellites,
the lot. (*Beat.*) Of course I will. (*She puts the phone down,
stands stock-still. Beat. She dials.*) You've not had a phone
call have you, Theresa, from the regiment? None of the
wives? (*Beat.*) It looks like it's a major one. (*Beat.*) I know, I
know… I can't help it, though. (*Beat.*) We would have heard
by now, surely? (*Beat.*) We would, wouldn't we, Theresa?
(*Beat.*) Okay. Let's just stay calm. (*Beat.*) I'll check the
website, for the list. (*Beat.*) Cheers. Yeah, but check every
hour, remember they add the names when… If you hear anything, ring me, and I'll do the same. Ta-ra, love.

*She puts the phone down. Goes straight to her laptop. Back
to watching the news.*

COLONEL WESTON *enters and stands to attention, he has
his back to us.* MRS WESTON *is still looking at the letter.
She touches some of her son's things. Looks at his photograph.* MAYA *enters and starts rummaging through a file.
She's on a mission.* MRS WESTON *opens the letter and
starts to read.*

MRS WESTON. Dear Sir. Mum. (*She catches her breath.*)

COLONEL WESTON. Don't, Olivia.

Beat. She looks at him.

Not now, darling. Another time perhaps, yes?

She looks at him and nods. She folds the letter and puts it back into the envelope with great care.

MRS WESTON. They were making a difference, weren't they?

COLONEL WESTON. Absolutely. Little by little, but… yes. Absolutely.

MRS WESTON. And he was happy? With the squadron?

COLONEL WESTON. He thought a great deal of those boys… they went through a lot together.

MRS WESTON. He never spoke about it to me. Ever.

COLONEL WESTON. Of course not. Why would he?

MRS WESTON. But… When he was younger… he used to tell me all sorts of things. What he was doing… things he wanted to do. Little secrets. I just wondered why…?

COLONEL WESTON. Probably wanted to protect you.

MRS WESTON. There isn't anything he could have said that would have been worse than what I was imagining. Every single day. (*She nearly breaks.*) I've been thinking about… that first Christmas he came home from school. Just after his seventh birthday. (*Beat.*) He was so happy to see me. He squeezed me so tight. He didn't want to go back, remember? (*Beat.*) But then, with every holiday… (*Beat.*) He was never that happy to see me again. I always hoped, wished… That that one time… that first time…

COLONEL WESTON. It doesn't help to dwell. We have to stay positive. For Andrew's sake. It's what he would have expected of us.

MRS WESTON *looks at the letter. She's desperate to continue reading it. Her husband takes it from her and puts it back into the box. Beat.*

I'd like you by my side for the press conference. Especially with the occasion and everything. They think it would be a good opportunity to... We'll put on a united front and set a bloody good example, eh, darling?

He leaves. Beat. Suddenly we are in a war zone. Chaos. Then one piercing, single scream.

Scene Four

GILL *is sat in the dark.* MIKE *enters.*

MIKE. What are you doing?

   GILL *switches a light on.*

GILL. I couldn't sleep. What are you doing up?

MIKE. Bad dream. The kids.

GILL. What was it about?

MIKE. Can't remember really. More of a feeling.

GILL. You've not called them kids for years. (*Beat.*) It wasn't about –

MIKE. No! (*Beat.*) I think... I thought someone was trying to get in the house. (*Beat.*) I couldn't move. I knew I had to protect us, but –

GILL. Oh, love, you're shaking. Come here.

   She holds him.

MIKE. What time is it? Is our Mikie home yet?

GILL. No. I've been sat here waiting for him. He'll have gone back to somebody's house for a few bevvies. He'll be in soon, don't worry.

MIKE. I'm not. (*Beat.*) Just nice knowing where they are, isn't it?

GILL. Yeah. He's a soldier, away for months on end, but when he's home... I can't rest until I hear his key in the door. Daft, isn't it?

MIKE. There's a lot of bloody nutters round here, nowadays. A few drinks inside them and they go mad. (*Beat.*) He'll probably crash over there, come home in the morning. Come back to bed.

Beat.

GILL. I might just sit here for a bit, love. I'll only keep you awake if I can't settle.

MIKE. Don't fall asleep sat there, or you'll end up with sore neck in the morning. (*He leaves.*)

The sound of BBC News 24 infiltrates the scene, gibberish with odd words, a foreign language, a recognisable word, getting louder and louder until GILL switches the TV on. Sound returns to normal.

Scene Five

MICHAEL *comes in from the pub. A* VOICE-OVER *starts speaking, mid-sentence.*

VOICE-OVER. ...American soldiers accused of raping an Iraqi girl and then murdering her and her family may have provoked the insurgent revenge plot in which two of their comrades were abducted and beheaded, it has been claimed –

MICHAEL. What you doing still up?

GILL. Shh.

MICHAEL *opens a bottle of beer and sits down.*

MICHAEL. Bloody hell, Mother, you're obsessed.

VOICE-OVER. Private Steven Green, twenty-one, recently discharged from the US army, appeared in an American federal court on murder and rape charges relating to her death. At least four other soldiers, still based in Iraq, are under investigation.

GILL. It's a terrible business this, isn't it?

MICHAEL. Is there any footie on?

He flicks the TV channel over. The occasional golf term can be heard.

Great. Hours of televised sky. (*He flicks through the channels.*) Any chance of a sarnie, Mum? Cheese on toast or something?

GILL goes to get him some food.

GILL (*as she goes*). Had a good night, love?

MICHAEL. Couple of pints in The Railway with Brownie and Yak and them lot, then back to Trab's for a game of poker.

GILL (*offstage*). How are they all doing?

MICHAEL. Same old, innit? Like havin' a moan but they don't wanna do anythin' about it, do they? Every day's the same. Stuck in some tedious job and struggling to get a 'foot on the ladder'. Would do my head in, that.

GILL comes in with slices of pizza. She strokes his hair.

GILL. There you go, cockle, how will cold pizza do you?

MICHAEL. Get in. Ta, Mum.

GILL takes the remote and changes the channel back to News 24. MICHAEL groans and gets stuck into his pizza.

GILL. Gives decent lads a bad name, that.

MICHAEL. What does?

GILL. This thing on the news. The Americans, the rape thing.

MICHAEL. What are you like! If you're not watching the telly, you're on the internet. You wanna chill out.

GILL. It puts me mind at rest. Especially when you're out there.

MICHAEL. It gets you all wound up, you mean. An' I'm here now, aren't I?

GILL. They deserve bloody floggin' for that, don't they?

MICHAEL. Who?

GILL. Them Americans.

MICHAEL. You only get half a story most of the time, all the sensational bits.

GILL. It is a bloody sensation.

MICHAEL. What I mean is that platoon might have taken a bad knock. (*He goes back to flicking through the channels.*) I wish me dad hadn't cancelled Sky Sports. He is one tight get!

Beat.

GILL. You can't just behave like savages, though, can you? Even in a war situation.

MICHAEL. Savages? (*Beat.*) Crime's simple there. Murders, theft, cut a hand off here, an ear there. They've got nothing… so they've got nothing to lose. (*Beat.*) They're not much into money-laundering or creaming off pension plans, like. Things can get pretty weird, know what I mean? Pretty 'savage' all round.

GILL. You're not trying to justify what them lads did, are you?

MICHAEL. I'm just saying I can understand how it could happen.

GILL. I can't believe you've just said that, Michael.

MICHAEL. You get nutjobs everywhere. Even in the army. And if you can't cope you don't get prescribed Prozac or anythin' like that, Mother. You just gotta get on with it. So? Life, innit?

GILL. Well, not in that case, no. Because of them two… murdering, raping… two of their own ended up paying the price. They were captured and beheaded in retaliation for what them two did. I'm telling you, they're savages.

MICHAEL. What constitutes a savage, then? The Iraqis don't use a machine to behead people, you know. They use knives. Knives that they use all the time. Not the sharpest tools, see what I'm saying? Cutting through some of the toughest bone

in the body. The skin, the flesh, the sinew, the base of the
skull. How long do you think that takes, eh? All that sawing
and grinding and screaming?

GILL. For God's sake, Michael, there's no need to –

MICHAEL. You can actually see stuff like that on the net...
There are videos passed around, Mother. That's what I'm
saying... it's not as simple as –

GILL. Granted, they should go through the proper channels,
that's what law and justice –

MICHAEL (*a pained laugh*). They would never report a sex
crime. They'd rather kill their own daughters than live with
the shame of people knowing she'd been raped. That's how
they think. Sounds mad to us, like. But they believe all that.
They have their own sense of justice. (*Beat.*) They're different to us. That's all.

GILL. But what about the legalities of war? The Geneva
Convention? What about that, then?

MICHAEL. You think that when someone's coming towards you
with a big fu... (*Stops himself from saying 'big fuck-off'.*) an
AKM rifle... you're gonna stop and think about the 'legalities' of war? Your head's in that moment, nowhere else!

GILL. I know you think I'm naïve. I probably am, but I still
think –

MICHAEL. I don't wanna argue with you, Mum. I'm just
saying... things are more complex than you might think.
(*Beat.*) They just are. (*Beat. He turns the TV off.*) I'm off up.

GILL (*quietly*). Michael, wait.

He stops but he doesn't look at her.

If they want to live in a democratic society, there has to be a
line drawn somewhere, doesn't there? I mean, that is what
we're trying to do out there, isn't it?

MICHAEL. Lines are drawn in offices, Mum, on paper, by
people with pens. For us, they get a little blurred sometimes.
(*Beat.*) Is our Chris in?

GILL. No… he's staying over at Kenny's. (*Beat.*) Do you think he's making a mistake?

MICHAEL. It's his life… his mistake, innit?

GILL. I wish he'd have listened to you, Michael.

MICHAEL. He's a man. It's what he wants.

GILL. You'll look out for him, won't you, love?

MICHAEL. It's not like… He'll probably be in a different company, might not even be in the same country. It depends.

GILL. No, but if you are… (*Beat.*) I'd feel better knowing that you'll be looking out for him. You will, won't you?

Beat.

MICHAEL. Yeah. Course I will.

He goes to her, hugs her, goes to pull away. She holds him a moment longer, squeezes him tight, then gets it together.

GILL. Shall I tell you something? You are the best of me. You and our Chris. All my good bits and none of the bad.

There is a moment between them. He pulls back.

MICHAEL. Should all go for an Indian or a Chinese or something before I go back. Few bevvies, an' that, just the four of us, eh?

GILL. That'll be nice. (*Beat.*) Go on, you go up. I'll follow in a minute, when I've locked up.

MICHAEL (*re: the TV*). Shouldn't dwell on stuff like that. Honest to God, Mum. They blow things out of all proportion. I'm telling you. It's dangerous. (*Beat.*) Night.

GILL. Goodnight, love.

He leaves. GILL *turns News 24 back on.* LUCY, MAYA *and* MRS WESTON *are in their own spaces, faces caught in a prism of thousands of blue-lit TV screens.*

Scene Six

Remembrance Sunday. Near the Cenotaph. COLONEL *and*
MRS WESTON *walk towards flashing cameras.* COLONEL
WESTON *has his arm around his wife's shoulder, proud,
smiling, assured. In contrast,* MRS WESTON's *smile looks on
the verge of madness, a caricature of pride and suppressed
grief.* MAYA *watches, across the divide.*

COLONEL WESTON. The British Army is one of the finest
forces in the world. Things change on a daily basis, but I...
my wife and I... have absolute confidence in the profession-
alism and dedication of our servicemen. From every rank.
(*Beat.*) We are very proud of what our boys are doing over
there. Very proud and moved at the dedication and determination to rebuild the infrastructure of a tragic country and our
son, Lieutenant Andrew Weston, assured us that the people of
Afghanistan more than welcomed that help. (*Beat.*) Darling?

Beat.

MRS WESTON. I am very proud of Andrew's achievements.
He was doing what he wanted to do. (*Beat.*) He spoke very
highly of the Afghani people. He'd even started to learn
Arabic. (*Beat. She looks at her husband.*) We are here today
to remember our son. And all the other servicemen who give
their lives on behalf of this great country.

COLONEL WESTON. Thank you. That is all.

As cameras flash he tries to usher his wife away. MAYA *con-
fronts them.*

MAYA. What about them that aren't remembered here today?
What about the soldiers who've been left on the scrapheap?
All the homeless ones, drunk in the gutter? They'll never
have their names on the Cenotaph.

The cameras turn to MAYA, *but she only sees* MRS
WESTON.

My son was in Kosovo with the UN. He came home a hero.
Proud. Because he knew he'd done something good there.

But after Iraq… (*Angrily.*) He deserves to be remembered. He loved being a soldier until…

COLONEL WESTON *tries to move his wife away.* MRS WESTON *is transfixed, watching* MAYA, *a safe distance away from the press.* MAYA *realises that she has the attention of the press. She tries to speak… can't… tries again… finally finds her voice.*

The second tour of Iraq finished my lad off. (*Beat.*) You could see it in… (*Beat.*) He had this puzzled look on his face… every time I saw him, it seemed to get worse. (*She breaks.*) He'd given sweets to a little girl playing in the street, and the next day he saw her body hanging from a tree… An Iraqi policeman told him not to give out any more sweets to the kids. He was a good son, a good husband and a good father… but he changed. I knew he needed help, but you don't ask for that sort of help in the army. The only thing he could do was get out. He loved the army, loved everything about it.

COLONEL WESTON *tries to get his wife to leave again, but she is still transfixed.*

I could see him and his wife, Sandra, were struggling. He came to stay with me for a bit. One morning I found him, sat on the bathroom floor, sobbing. I said, 'You can't go into work in that state.' He was relieved. 'Thank you, thank you, Mum', over and over. 'Thank you.' (*Beat.*) Two days later I found him in the garage, sat in the car in his uniform. (*Beat.*) When the hospital gave us his things back, we found… He'd stuffed his pockets with all these leaflets. Post-Traumatic Stress Syndrome. He'd never mentioned it to any of us. Not one word. (*Beat.*) My son was as much a casualty of this war as (MRS WESTON.) that woman's there. But he won't be remembered at the Cenotaph because he didn't die in action. If it's the last thing I do… I'll scratch his name onto it. They can put me away for it, I don't care. His name was Sergeant Joseph Johnson.

A bell. She unfolds a banner for Military Families Against the War. A sea of camera flashes.

Military Families are here to make sure that our troops are brought home and taken care of properly.

MAYA *is manhandled away.*

(*Shouting.*) And I'm gonna make sure that every soldier who gives his life for this country will never be forgotten.

MAYA*'s voice segues into a radio broadcast, as she reads out the names of the dead. A* NEWSCASTER *speaks over* MAYA*'s protest.*

NEWSCASTER. There were dramatic scenes at the Cenotaph today. Just before the Queen and members of the Royal Family arrived for the Armistice Parade, Maya Johnson, the mother of an ex-soldier who committed suicide last year after completing two tours of Iraq, managed to break security to speak on behalf of Military Families Against the War. Mrs Johnson is aggrieved that her son, a sergeant who served with the 2nd Tank Regiment for fourteen years, is not formally entitled to be remembered at the Cenotaph as he was a civilian at the time of his death. Members of the government were informed of the breach of security –

MAYA. Kelan John Turrington, eighteen.

Bell.

Lance Corporal Ian Malone, twenty-eight.

Bell.

Piper Christopher Muzvuru, twenty-one.

Bell.

Lieutenant Alexander Tweedie, twenty-five.

Bell.

Lance Corporal James McCue, twenty-seven.

NEWSCASTER. After her arrest, a police spokesperson said that Mrs Johnson had met with army officials on several occasions to discuss her son's case. No civilian is entitled to have their... (*His voice fades.*)

Scene Seven

CHRIS *sits at a PlayStation.*

CHRIS. Come on, you little towel-headed, camel-jockey cunt, ya. Just give me one pop. One little pop. (*Beat.*) Come on, baby, a clean shot at your ugly fuckin' durka-durka kite an' we're outta here.

GILL *enters.*

GILL. Are you still stuck on that bloody stupid thing?

CHRIS (*misses a clear shot*). Cheers, Mum. I near had him, then.

GILL. The taxi's due in about ten minutes. Our Michael's moaning about the creases in his brand-new shirt and your dad's on the phone. There's only me ready to go. You've not even got your shoes on.

CHRIS. Bleedin' hell, Ma. / I'll wear me trabs.

GILL. Don't call me 'Ma', it sounds common. And you are not wearing your trainers.

CHRIS. I didn't even wanna go.

GILL. Well, don't come, if you feel like that. (*Beat.*) Be nice for us all to have a meal together before our Michael goes back and you go away, that's all.

She starts ironing MICHAEL's *shirt.*

CHRIS. Then why can't we just do that? Why does it have to be some big friggin' poncy 'do', where we've all gotta get dressed up? Why do we have to be told what to wear?

GILL. God, if that's what's worrying you then you'd better get used to it. They tell you what to wear all the time in the army.

CHRIS. It's not the same. A uniform is not the same as getting all ponced up when you're not in the mood.

GILL. Do you know what, Christopher, you've got a lot to learn, you have.

CHRIS. Yeah, yeah. Here we go.

GILL. I'm just saying, get used to doing stuff that you're 'not in the mood' for because once that lot tell you to jump, you're gonna have to jump. Sharpish.

CHRIS. Alright, alright. Back off, will you!

GILL. Don't you raise your voice to me.

CHRIS. Then get off me case.

GILL. I'm only pointing out that –

CHRIS. Stop telling me what to do. I'm sick of having to answer to people all the time! Where I go, who I go with, what time I'm gonna be back. Now you're tryin'a tell me what to wear. Why don't you just have me tagged? The army will be a breeze compared to living here.

GILL. Oh, you reckon, do you? You don't know you're bloody born, lad. What we do for you. Every day.

CHRIS. Don't do it, then. I never ask you, do I?

GILL. Oh, forget it. Let's not bother going, eh? Let's do everything to suit Christopher.

CHRIS. If I didn't go, our Mikie wouldn't mind. Me dad wouldn't mind. It's you that's done all the organising. This is all for you, this, not us.

GILL. It was our Michael, actually. He suggested it. He's your brother and he'll be going back to a bloody war zone in a couple of days. The least we can do is give him a decent send-off.

CHRIS. Why does everything have to turn into one big massive deal in this house?

GILL. Oh, go and tell your dad and our Michael that you don't want to go, then. I'll phone the restaurant and cancel the table.

CHRIS. I didn't say I didn't want to go, did I? I just don't want you gettin' on me case over petty nonsense. (*Beat*.) Have you seen me shoes?

GILL. Where did you leave them?

CHRIS. If I knew that, I wouldn't be asking had you seen them, would I?

GILL (*puts her hand over her eyes*). One's on the bathroom floor, looking all forlorn and confused, wondering how the hell it got there, while the other is in the conservatory, under the table. Just where you kicked it off. Probably. (*Beat. She clicks her fingers.*) You're back in the room.

CHRIS. That's really hilarious, that, you should be on the stage. 'Ma.'

GILL. Try getting off your backside and looking for them, eh, Christopher?

MICHAEL (*offstage*). What are you doing, slinging that over the chair, you bleedin' idiot. That's four hundred quid's worth of Paul Smith, that jacket.

MIKE (*offstage*). What did you leave it hanging over the door for, then, soft lad? I couldn't open the bloody thing cause of the hanger.

CHRIS. I'll stick me trainers on –

MICHAEL (*offstage*). You could have just moved it like that –

GILL. You will not. It's a nice restaurant, you'll put your shoes on –

MIKE (*offstage*). – and you could have used a bit of sense and left it hanging up in your wardrobe till you were ready to put the bloody thing on –

MICHAEL (*offstage*). Alright, alright, don't be throwin' an eppie. 'Kin 'ell.

GILL (*calling*). Do you two want to shout louder so them three doors down can hear you?

CHRIS (*still looking for his shoes*). I'm gonna have to wear me trainies.

GILL. They've got to be here somewhere, Christopher –

MIKE *enters*.

CHRIS. It's only a bloody restaurant, for Christ's sake, what's the big deal –

MIKE. Hey! Don't you be starting. There's one out there, thinking he's mouth-almighty, we could do without the matching pair, ta very much.

CHRIS. I don't believe this. I'm just sat playing a game, happy, doing nothin' wrong, when suddenly it all kicks off an' now I'm in the middle of World War Three!

GILL. Alright, alright, Al Pacino, you can stop the overacting. Mike, have you seen his shoes?

MIKE. They're on the back step.

CHRIS. What? What are they doing out there?

MIKE. I give them a bit of a polish for you.

CHRIS (*leaving*). Oh, right. Cheers.

GILL (*leaving*). I've got to iron our Michael's brand-new shirt 'cause he doesn't like the creases down the arms, and you're cleaning his bloody shoes for him.

MIKE. 'And the enemy, they do tremble.' Christ on a friggin' skateboard. There's not an ounce of common sense between the pair of them. If Osama Bin Laden's cronies had any idea what they were up against, they'd come out of their caves, stop the training and go on an all-inclusive to Dubai for a few weeks.

MICHAEL *comes in, bare-chested.*

MICHAEL (*calling*). Cheers, Mum, you're an angel.

GILL (*offstage*). Well, don't be complaining if it's not perfect. I know what you're like.

MICHAEL (*calling*). It's just the creases, everything else is alright. (*To himself.*) She is really shit at ironing.

CHRIS *enters, carrying his shoes.*

CHRIS (*to* MICHAEL). Put it away, you're knocking me sick.

MICHAEL (*flexing his muscles*). You wish you had half of what I've got going on here, lad.

CHRIS. Is it, yeah?

MICHAEL. Pure muscle, mate. A lean, mean, sex machine. Watch and weep. (*He poses.*)

MIKE. Behave. Both of youse spend that much time in the bathroom, you're worse than a pair of girls. (*He leaves.*)

MICHAEL. Don't be comparing my twelve-and-a-half stone of pure throbbing power to that feeble attempt at masculinity. Seen more meat on a butcher's pencil.

CHRIS. What's size got to do with it? It's the shape you're in, innit?

MICHAEL. That's what I'm saying, you're gonna have to work hard at getting anywhere near this, lad.

CHRIS. Ya cheeky get. I'm as fit as you.

MICHAEL (*laughing*). Stop chanting rubbish.

CHRIS. I told you. I got one of the highest scores in me physical. I've been training, running, on the weights. (*He poses.*) Telling you.

MICHAEL. Here are then, hit the floor. (*Throws himself on the floor and gets ready to do press-ups.*)

CHRIS. Got me good gear on, haven't I?

MICHAEL. Scared I'm gonna give you a beasting? (*Beat. Imitating him.*) 'I've been training.'

Beat. CHRIS *takes his shirt off and gets down.*

CHRIS. Go head then. Press-up wars.

MICHAEL. Press-ups wars? Ooooooh. (*Beat.*) Come on then. Let's rock, motherfucker.

MIKE (*offstage*). Stop acting like a pair of bloody kids, the taxi will be here shortly.

They start the press-up war, trying to pull each other's arm from under them. GILL *comes in.*

GILL. What are you doing?

The lads are really going for it.

MIKE (*passing through*). Acting daft. Neither of them is right in the head. (*He leaves.*)

GILL. You've only just got out the shower! Stop messing about and get up.

The lads are focused on each other, really trying to win.

MICHAEL. Ha-ha. Nearly had you there, didn't I?

CHRIS. But you didn't, did you?

GILL. Will you stop it, please, and get up! I mean it.

MICHAEL. He's in the army now, Mum, he's learning to play with the big boys.

CHRIS. Are there any big boys here, then?

GILL (*calling*). Mike? Will you get in here and tell these two, please?

MIKE (*offstage*). Ignore them. They're like a pair of soddin' toddlers when they get in that mood.

CHRIS *knocks* MICHAEL's *hand away.* MICHAEL *recovers and they continue. Now it's serious.*

CHRIS. Woohoo! Didn't like that, did you?

MICHAEL. That all you've got? Go head.

They are two men, in combat. A couple of near-misses on either side.

GILL (*shouting*). Pack it in, now! I mean it. If you don't pack it in, I'll pack it in for you. (*Beat.*) I mean it. Michael? Christopher. Stop it. Right.

GILL *bends down to try physically to stop them.* CHRIS *knocks* MICHAEL's *arm from underneath him, he collapses.*

CHRIS. Yes! Yes! Yes!

MICHAEL (*tries to take a 'half-hearted' pop at* CHRIS). Come on, she got in the way –

GILL. Who's 'she'? The cat's mother?

A bit of a scuffle between them. MIKE *comes in just as* CHRIS *takes a pop at* MICHAEL. GILL *reacts, gets in between.*

MIKE. Hey, hey, hey! What the bloody hell's going on!

GILL. I could see this coming!

The brothers glare at each other, ready to kill. A moment of utter terror for the whole family. It could go either way.

MIKE (*quietly. Aware of the power in the room*). Don't even think about it. Either of you.

Beat.

GILL. Michael? Christopher?

MICHAEL (*relaxing*). Chill out!

He grabs CHRIS *and rustles his hair.* CHRIS *pulls away.*

We were only messing. (*To* CHRIS.) Weren't we?

Beat. CHRIS *nods.*

What's up with youse all!

MICHAEL *jumps to his feet. Offers his brother a hand up.*

Beat. CHRIS *takes it.*

GILL. Don't put that shirt on until you've stopped sweating. And you, get them shoes on. Now.

CHRIS. Alright, alright. Keep your hair on.

They dress in silence. GILL *and* MIKE *watch them. Beat.*

MICHAEL. How am I lookin'?

MIKE. A lot less than four hundred quid.

MICHAEL. Cheeky get. There's just under a grand in bling alone here, mate.

GILL. You look lovely. You both do.

Beat.

MICHAEL. Looking forward to this. I'm starving, could eat a scabby rat. (*Beat. To* CHRIS.) What about you, mate? (*Beat.*) We'll have to make sure we put a good lining on, with the scran, eh?

GILL. What are you on about?

CHRIS. We're off into town after the meal.

MIKE. Who is?

CHRIS. Us is. Me an' him.

Beat.

MIKE. Up to you, isn't it? Do what you want.

GILL. Where did I put me digital camera? I had it in me hand not five minutes ago.

A taxi beeps.

MIKE. There's the taxi.

GILL. Hang on, I want to take a photo of the four of us before we go. Where's me digital camera?

MICHAEL. Sod that, Mother. We've done enough faffin', let's just go.

CHRIS. Seconded.

The lads leave.

GILL. Hang on. It'll take me two minutes to find the digital camera. (*Calling.*) Two minutes.

MAYA *and* LUCY *enter. The following scene overlaps, but shouldn't intrude on the rhythm of* MIKE *and* GILL *leaving.*

MIKE. We don't need any more soddin' photos, Gill, we know what they bloody look like. Come on, he'll be charging us waiting time if we don't hurry up. (*Beat.*) The robbing dog.

He goes. For a moment, the three MOTHERS *are together.* GILL *leaves.*

Scene Eight

LUCY *and* MAYA *sit, talking. Kate Bush is on in the background.*

LUCY. Will you stop beating yourself up over it, Maya?

MAYA. I just saw red and went for it.

LUCY. You don't have to explain yourself to me.

MAYA. Kadife wasn't very happy with me, though –

LUCY. Kadife can mind her own business. She's used to this game, we're only getting started.

MAYA. Yeah, but she does have a point. I mean, Remembrance Sunday? Probably done more damage than good.

LUCY. You're getting boring now. Let's open a bottle of wine and forget about all that lot for a bit.

LUCY *gets a bottle of wine. Kate Bush's 'Army Dreamers' comes on. Beat. They laugh.*

Sorry, Kate. You're great, but not tonight, eh? (*She turns it off.*) What are we in the mood for?

MAYA. Something with a bit of soul. Something a bit sexy.

LUCY. Okay. You open the wine and I'll find us something nice. The corkscrew is over there.

MAYA *looks for the corkscrew. She picks up a tube of athlete's foot cream. And another, and another.*

MAYA. Is this to send out to your Greg?

LUCY. His feet are in a state, their boots are melting in the heat. I can't imagine what they smell like. When he's here, I make him leave his trainers on the back step.

MAYA. There must be about seventy quid's worth there! It'll take him months to get through all that!

LUCY. It's not just for him. (*Beat*). Here we are. Marvin Gaye.

MAYA *looks through the boxes of foot cream,* LUCY *puts Marvin Gaye on. Beat.*

He'll have to share it with his mates, won't he?

Beat. As the beautiful voice of Marvin Gaye sings 'What's Happening Brother', MAYA sighs.

MAYA. Never stops, does it? There's always something.

LUCY. What's wrong? What is it?

MAYA. It's Sandra, our Joe's wife. (*Beat.*) She's on about moving away. I don't know what I'll do if she does, I love them two kids. I can't imagine not being able to see them whenever I want to. She's just doing what she thinks is right for them. It's understandable, I suppose. In the circumstances.

Beat.

LUCY. Has something happened?

MAYA. She saw the news. (*Beat.*) We had words. She said it was the last straw.

LUCY. The last straw?

MAYA. I 'embarrass her', apparently. She says I need to 'move on'. I tried to explain to her how I feel. How I can't sit back any more, but she doesn't get it. All this campaigning, me getting arrested. She said if I carry on, it might affect the kids. (*Beat.*) I understand it's difficult for her, we all have to deal with things in our own way, but she shouldn't use the kids against me.

LUCY. Our Greg put the phone down on me last night. Couple of the lads have been winding him up. He'll calm down, he always does. He'll e-mail me later in the week. All we can do is do what we think is right. (*Beat.*) Hey, I thought you sounded great on the telly, though.

MAYA. I didn't go with the intention of actually talking. It was that Mrs Weston. Smiling for the cameras, next to her husband in his uniform. It got me all wound up. (*Beat.*) Lucy?

LUCY. What?

MAYA. I'd rather know the truth, so just be honest with me. (*Beat.*) Did I look fat on the telly?

Beat. They fall about laughing, then join in with Marvin Gaye, joyous. They carry on with the parcel.

Scene Nine

Chaos as MICHAEL *and* CHRIS *stagger down the street.* MICHAEL *shouts off,* CHRIS *tries to restrain him.*

MICHAEL. Let go of me. I'll fuckin' have him, I'm tellin' ya, he's mine.

CHRIS. Will you keep your voice down? You're gonna wake the whole street up, ya tube.

MICHAEL. I'm goin' back an' havin' him. Startin' on you like that. Nobody talks to you like that.

He tries to go back to the 'fight'. CHRIS *holds on to him.*

CHRIS. It wasn't him, it was you.

MICHAEL *sits on the floor.*

I know him, he's a good lad, he was just letting on to us. He was bevvied, is all.

MICHAEL. What was he laughin' at, then? Eh? What the fuck was all that about?

CHRIS. Being pissed-up, that's what. Jesus. (*Beat.*) You just zoned in on him, like a fuckin' meff. If I hadn't have been there –

MICHAEL. You're my brother an' I'm not gonna stand by and watch some fuckin' Paki take the rip out of you –

CHRIS. He's not a Paki, well, he is, he's from Sri Lanka, but he's sound, he's me mate, ya knob –

MIKE (*coming out*). What the bloody hell?… Christ… help us get him in before he wakes the whole soddin' street up.

MIKE *and* CHRIS *struggle with* MICHAEL. *He doesn't know where he is. He takes a half-hearted swing out.*

MICHAEL. Don't smirk at him, I'll fuckin' take the lot of youse.

CHRIS *gets in between them;* MICHAEL *is blindly swinging at the pair of them.* MIKE *is trying to dodge him,* CHRIS *is interjecting, screaming for* MICHAEL *to come to and see sense.*

CHRIS. It's me and me dad, ya tube!

GILL *enters. Watches, from a distance.* MICHAEL *'comes to'. He laughs.*

MICHAEL. Sorry, Dad. Sorry, Mum. Waking you up.

They struggle to get him inside.

Out of order. Bang out of order. Home. That's where we're going. Can't beat it. Where the heart is, innit? Get us home, Chris.

CHRIS. You stupid get. We are home, we're in the house. Come on, get upstairs.

MIKE *helps* CHRIS *with* MICHAEL.

MICHAEL (*sees* GILL, *staring at him. He's pissed-up, getting sentimental*). Mum, I love you. Love you an' all, Dad. You're me family, only thing that's important. Chris, you know that, don't you? Tell 'em what's important. Tell them. You know that, don't you?

CHRIS. I know that you're making a tit of yourself when you should just shurrup and get up these stairs.

MICHAEL. That poem? What's that poem?

GILL. Michael, please go to bed, it's late.

MICHAEL. Think he was Welsh. Queer. Ages ago, ages ago.

CHRIS. What are you on about?

MICHAEL. The poem. What's wrong with youse?

MIKE. You are what's wrong with us, Mikie. Talking shite, when you've had a drink, as per.

MICHAEL. Sorry, sorry. But these things are important, aren't they? (*Beat*.) Doesn't matter that he was queer. Was just telling the truth, wasn't he?

They lead him off. CHRIS *fetches a bucket of water.* MIKE *barks out an order, in the voice of a brutal sergeant.*

MIKE. Sort yourself out, lad.

Everyone reacts. MICHAEL *sticks his head in the bucket.* CHRIS *starts to get changed.*

Scene Ten

MRS WESTON *tries to read her son's letter.*

MRS WESTON. We didn't really get to know each other as much as I would have liked. I regret that, truly I do. It is not so unusual and certainly not a reflection of how much I care for you both. We simply didn't take the time to talk. No recriminations, just the way it was. Now, when I'm sure you are both trying to come to terms with the news of my death, I want to take this time to let you know a little bit more about me. I hope it helps.

She can't read any more.

Scene Eleven

Through the grainy image of a video-camera, we see a passing out parade. The other MOTHERS *walk forward, proud, formal, and proceed to dress* CHRIS *in his uniform. When he is ready,* MRS WESTON *puts the finishing touches, with a kiss and a stroke of his hair.* CHRIS *looks fantastic in his uniform.* GILL *and* MIKE *take photos and fuss around him. There are other people, equally proud and happy.*

GILL. Let me get one of you two, here, under this tree.

MIKE. You don't want me to emphasise what an ugly bugger he is, do ya?

CHRIS *puts his arm around his dad.* GILL *takes the photo.*

CHRIS. It's bleedin' hot, isn't it? (*He signals to one of the lads.*) Alright, B.S.?

MIKE. B.S.? What's that short for?

CHRIS. Dave.

MIKE. Dave?

CHRIS. He says 'basically speaking' all the time, so he gets called 'B.S.' for short.

MIKE. Right.

GILL. B.S. isn't shorter than Dave, is it?

CHRIS. Forget it, Mother. (*Beat.*) Our Mikie rang me the other day. He was only on a couple of minutes.

GILL. Tuesday? He was on to us on Tuesday, wasn't he? Well, your dad spoke to him, I was out. What was he saying?

CHRIS (*looking at his dad*). The usual, you know. (*Beat.*) Askin' how it was going, an' that. He –

GILL. You look just like him in your uniform.

MIKE (*laughing*). Sod off. He's not as good-looking as our Michael! –

CHRIS. Ya cheeky get –

GILL. They're both good-looking.

CHRIS. He's windin' you up, Mum, take no notice. (*Beat.*) But I don't look anything like our Mikie, now, do I?

GILL. I mean, in your uniform. All tall and straight. You can tell you're brothers, that's all I meant.

MIKE. You could say that about the whole bloody platoon on parade then, ya daft sod.

GILL. No. No. I could easy pick our Michael and Christopher out of the whole regiment if I had to.

MIKE *and* CHRIS *laugh*.

Do you know what...?

MIKE. Where are the loos?

CHRIS. See that building there? Just at the back of there, green door.

MIKE *leaves*.

GILL. So? You did it, didn't ya, kiddo.

CHRIS. Yep.

GILL. I'll be honest with you, Christopher. I didn't think it'd be your thing. You never liked doing as you were told, when you were little. I'm proud you've stuck with it, love. Really proud.

CHRIS. Cheers, Mum. (*Beat*.) It was touch-an'-go at first, like. You get some right bastards here. Nasty, cruel bastards. But once you get into the swing of things... It's about guts, innit? What you can take an' how you can handle it. (*Beat*.) Makes you feel... dunno... The mates you make in here... there's nothin' like them. (*Beat*.) Should have done it when I first left school. (*Beat*.) I'm lovin' it, Mum, honest. Absolutely loving it.

GILL. That'll do for me.

Beat.

CHRIS. Our Mikie didn't seem himself, you know, the other day.

GILL. What do you mean?

CHRIS. Bit distant. I couldn't get a proper conversation out of him.

GILL. Your dad never said anything. Had he had a drink?

CHRIS. Probably. (*Beat*.) I don't think it's anything to worry about, like. (*Beat*.) He's heard that Sarah's got a new fella.

GILL. Well, that was bound to happen, wasn't it?

CHRIS. Thing is… he was a bit pissed off with me, about it all.

GILL. With you? Why?

CHRIS. Because when he was at home, I told him I'd bumped into her. And he… well, he more or less asked me if she was with anyone. I blagged him and said I didn't know. (*Beat*.) What was I supposed to do? He'd only been home five minutes; I didn't want to put a dampener on things.

GILL. Don't worry, love, he'd understand.

CHRIS. Yeah, I know, but – (*Beat*.) Just got a bad vibe from him. It's not like our Mikie to take off on us like that.

GILL. Funny your dad didn't say anything.

CHRIS. Probably not had that much sleep or something. You know what our Mikie's like without his kip.

GILL. You didn't have a proper fall-out with him, did you?

CHRIS. No! He was just a bit… weird with me, that's all.

GILL. Weird in what way?

CHRIS. Ripping me. About me trainin'. Me running times… that sort of stuff. He said it's easier now, the physicals and that. Said I might as well have joined the Boy Scouts.

GILL. He'll have been winding you up… he won't have meant anything by it, love.

CHRIS. It's not a competition, though, is it? (*Beat*.) I thought he'd be dead proud of me.

GILL. Of course he's proud of you.

CHRIS. Yeah, well, ripping into me training took the shine off it a bit. I don't think there was any need for that.

MIKE *enters*.

GILL. Was our Michael alright the other day? Our Chris said he had a face on him. How did he sound to you?

MIKE. He was shattered, that's all. They get days like that. There's nothing to worry about, for God's sake.

GILL. Are you sure?

MIKE. I'd say if there was, wouldn't I?

GILL. Well, I'd hope so.

MIKE *gives* CHRIS *daggers. Beat.*

CHRIS. Probably just pissed off about Sarah, hey?

MIKE. Are we gonna manage to get a pint in today, or what?

GILL (*to* CHRIS). He'd have been messing, I'm telling you.
Don't be worrying, you. (*Beat.*) That Sarah one, eh? She
always thought she was a cut above. That's the last thing he
needs when he's out there. She wasn't right for our Michael,
I knew that, from day one. Hey, and he wants to get that
juicer back off her. I paid forty-odd quid for that, last
Christmas, for her. And that was with ten per cent off, from
our Ann's fella.

MIKE. What the bloody hell has the juicer got to do with
anything?

GILL. He's too soft, our Michael, he always has been. Letting
people walk all over him.

CHRIS. Don't say anything, Mum. I don't want him to think
I've been talking about him.

MIKE. You have, though, haven't you?

CHRIS. You know what I mean.

GILL. Where are the loos, again?

MIKE. Back of that building, green door.

GILL *leaves.*

MIKE. What the bloody hell did you say anything to her about
that for, ya dickhead? He might just be a bit down, you know
what she's like. That's why I kept schtum. There's no point
giving her anything else to worry about, is there? Our
Michael doesn't want her knowing all the ins and outs. She'd
be a bag of bloody nerves. Honestly, Chris, you want to learn
to think before you open your mouth sometimes, Jesus.

CHRIS. Alright, alright. (*Beat.*) Anyway… I've got some news of me own. I'm not gonna say anything to her today, like, but… We've been given our orders. (*Beat.*) Gonna be joining our Michael for a bit… then we might be off to Afghanistan.

MIKE. What? (*Beat.*) Christ, they don't mess about, do they? Bloody hell, Chris. (*Beat.*) Caught me a bit off-guard with that one. I didn't expect… So soon, like –

CHRIS. It's what we've been gearing up for, though, isn't it? These past couple of months, an' that. The lads are made up. (*Beat.*) Think about it. Best to go now when everything's fresh, stuck in here. (*His head.*) When we know what we're doing. (*Beat.*) Can't fuckin' wait, Dad. Honest.

An imam's call to prayer over a beautiful sunset.

Scene Twelve

All the MOTHERS *walk forward. The imam's call gets louder. The bells get louder. On screen, we see people answer the imam's call, kneeling in prayer, a ritual at a mosque; holy, ancient, beautiful. The* MOTHERS *are transfixed. Each performs their own little ritual of safekeeping. Beat.* MRS WESTON *tunes the radio in.* LUCY *sits at a laptop.* MAYA *sorts through leaflets for Military Families Against the War.* GILL *is making up a parcel of things for her boys.* MIKE *is sat reading the paper. Everyone tunes in to the same thing, underscoring the action.*

GILL. Do you want a cup of tea, love?

MIKE. No thanks.

GILL. It's funny without him, isn't it?

MIKE. That's about the third time you've said that.

GILL. I'm used to our Michael not being here but I can't seem to get used to our Chris being away. Under me feet.

MIKE. He's only been gone a few weeks, you best get used to it.

Beat.

GILL. Don't you miss him, Mike?

MIKE. Of course I bloody miss him. But there's no point banging on about it, is there? What can we do?

GILL. I'm just saying! It's alright to say that we miss him, isn't it?

MIKE (*sighing*). But why waste time banging on about it? We can't change it, can we?

GILL. No need to bite me head off. (*Beat.*) He seemed a bit cheerier the other night, didn't he? Our Michael, I mean?

MIKE. Yep. (*Beat.*) I think I'll nip down The Railway for a quick one.

GILL. Aw don't, Mike. It's only half past two.

MIKE. So? It's Saturday, isn't it? If I was working, this would be me day off. (*Beat.*) Come with us if you fancy. I'll just stick a clean shirt on.

He leaves. A newsflash. GILL *turns the TV up. A* NEWSCASTER *reports. Throughout the following, the* MOTHERS *are attentive to their own way of seeing or hearing the report.*

NEWSCASTER. The attack took place in the early hours of this morning, just south of Basra. Five British soldiers and an Iraqi interpreter were killed. Three British soldiers were also wounded –

GILL. Where's this? (*Shouting.*) Mike? Mike, come down a minute –

NEWSCASTER. – when a fierce battle broke out. It is believed the patrol was ambushed by insurgents –

GILL (*shouting*). Mike?

NEWSCASTER. – The soldiers were part of a Light Aid Detachment unit for the 1st Royal Tank Regiment. The patrol had been taking part in an operation to help widen irrigation ditches when they were ambushed –

MIKE *enters*.

MIKE. What's up?

GILL. Listen –

NEWSCASTER. – In a separate incident, four soldiers were killed just north of Helmand when a roadside bomb exploded. The area is known locally as the 'desert of death', a stark landscape of burned flats and scorching heat, with dust storms an almost daily occurrence –

LUCY stands. She knows it's her boy.

We'll bring you the latest on that as soon as we can. (*Beat.*) Gordon Brown visited Edinburgh today to open a new wing of the…

GILL flicks through the channels for more news. MAYA watches LUCY. MRS WESTON sits.

MIKE. Let's not panic, eh? There are a hell of a lot of soldiers based there.

GILL. He mentioned the LAD. With the 1st Royal Tank Regiment.

MIKE. Put News 24 on. (*Beat.*) When did it happen?

GILL. Early hours.

News 24 are talking world markets.

Shit. (*Beat.*) I'm gonna phone him. (*She dials on her mobile.*)

MIKE. There's no point. You heard what the fella on the news said. There'll be no getting through until they've done what they've got to do.

GILL. I don't care. I can still try. (*Beat.*) It's gone straight to answermachine.

MIKE. I told you.

There's a knock on the door. All the MOTHERS react. Beat.

GILL (*quietly*). Don't open it, Mike.

MIKE. It's alright, it's alright. Sit down. Stop jumping to conclusions. (*He doesn't move.*) It could be anybody, that. Probably Tony calling on the off-chance.

GILL. Don't open the door, please. It's our Michael, it's our Michael.

More insistent knocking.

(*Whispering.*) Please God no, please God no, please God no.

MIKE. Stop it! (*He goes to her.*) Come on now. It's alright. (*Beat.*) I'm gonna open the door, Gill.

GILL *shakes her head.*

Listen to me. It's okay. There's nothing to worry about. Are you listening, hey? There's someone at the front door, just like loads of times before so... I'm going to open it, okay? Alright? (*Beat.*) We're alright, aren't we, love?

GILL *nods.*

See. We're alright. We're alright. (*Beat.*) It could be anybody that, couldn't it? Okay. I'm going to open that door.

He goes to open the front door. GILL *sits still, holding her breath.* MAYA *goes to* LUCY, *puts her arm around her. All the* MOTHERS *are terrified of the knocking.* LUCY *buries her head into* MAYA's *shoulder.* MRS WESTON *can't bear it. It's the moment when the other* MOTHERS *are told about the death of their sons.*

MIKE (*whispering, to himself*). Please God. Jesus. Allah. Buddha. Whoever's out there... take me instead of one of them. Even if you're the devil. Take me.

GILL. It's just Tony, calling on the off-chance. It's just Tony, it's just Tony.

Beat. He opens the door. Blackout.

End of Act One.

ACT TWO

Scene One

CHRIS *comes running on with* GILL *over his shoulder. He's in uniform.* MICHAEL *is sat at the table, a suitcase at his feet. He's also in uniform. He doesn't react to* GILL *and* CHRIS.

CHRIS. Is it, yeah? Gonna make us all giddy, is it, Ma? All light-headed, like this?

He spins her round and round. He laughs at GILL's *mock protests.*

GILL. Stop it, you swine, you. Tell him, Mike. Chris, put me down, you daft sod. Will you stop it! I'll swing for you, Chris. I'm warning you. I'm not messing. Mike? Tell him.

CHRIS *puts her down.* GILL *smacks him away, and sits down.*

Honest to God, you can be one annoying little get when you want to, Christopher.

CHRIS (*turns and watches the scene*). As if I'd ever let you fall. As if I'd ever let you fall.

GILL *stays with the memory for a moment.* MICHAEL *touches her hand, she returns to 'now' with a jolt.*

GILL. It's funny this time. (*Beat.*) You coming home, wearing your uniform.

MICHAEL. Latest fad, innit? 'Wear it with pride.' It's a joke.

GILL. But you do look very handsome in it.

GILL *looks at the laptop.* MIKE *comes in with a can of beer for* MICHAEL.

MIKE. There you go, lad, get that down you.

MICHAEL. Bit early, innit?

MIKE. It's a welcome-home drink. It's good to see you.

MICHAEL. Cheers, Dad. (*Beat*.) Want to join us, Mum? A glass of wine or something?

GILL. Not for me, love.

MIKE *and* MICHAEL *look at each other.*

MIKE. Don't be daft. You can't not join us in a celebration drink for our Mikie coming home.

MICHAEL. No worries, Dad. We can all go down The Railway or something tonight, if you fancy.

GILL. I suppose a little one won't –

MIKE. She can just have a little one –

GILL. That's what I just said, isn't it?

Beat.

They all drink in silence.

MIKE. Three weeks, eh? They've given you a good stint this time, haven't they, kiddo?

MICHAEL. Yeah. (*Beat*.) Might go down south for a couple of days next week, though… see some of the lads, an' that.

MIKE. It's your leave, mate, you take it easy. You deserve it. (*Beat*.) We're just glad to have you back home. Aren't we, Gill?

GILL. Course we are.

MICHAEL. How's Tony doing?

MIKE. Alright –

GILL. We hardly ever see him.

MIKE. I wouldn't say hardly ever… He's got a lot on, that's all.

GILL. I can't remember the last time he was round here. Can you?

Beat.

MICHAEL. Something smells good. It's not lamb, is it? Say it's lamb, Mum, please.

GILL. It's lamb.

MICHAEL *tries, half-heartedly, to pick his mum up. She doesn't protest or join in with the joke.*

MICHAEL. Get in! Been dreaming about that for weeks.

GILL. It's your favourite, isn't it?

MICHAEL (*singing*). 'She knows me so well.'

GILL. He's making it, I just bought it.

Beat.

MICHAEL. Well, I can't wait.

MIKE (*to* MICHAEL). You won't have to, it's nearly done, lad.

GILL. To tell you the truth. (*Beat.*) I'm not that hungry, you know.

MIKE. Don't be daft –

GILL. Might wait and have some later, Mike.

Beat. GILL *looks at her laptop.*

MIKE. Wastes a hell of a lot of leccy on standby like that, all day. You should be thinking about your carbon footprint.

GILL. I haven't finished on it yet.

Beat.

MIKE. I'll go an' sort the gravy out. The roasties are nearly done. (*Beat.*) Want me to put you a little plate out anyway, just in case –

GILL. I can't eat if I'm not hungry, can I?

MIKE *leaves. Beat.*

MICHAEL. State of him, Gordon bleedin' Ramsay, eh? (*Beat.*) He'll be walking around in an apron next.

GILL. He's into it. Seems to enjoy it.

Beat.

MICHAEL. Take it he's still not found anything, then?

GILL. Nope.

MICHAEL. I thought Tony was gonna put a word in for him, at his place?

GILL. Tony was all talk. (*Beat.*) Like a lot of them. He's on about going on the taxis.

MICHAEL. 'Im? The taxis?

GILL. That's his latest thing, yep.

The laptop beeps a mail alert. She goes to it. Beat.

MICHAEL (*trying for an effort at familial normality*). So… what's all this then, Mum? What are you doing?

He looks at her research. It's a disappointment.

GILL. This is the stuff I was telling you about.

MICHAEL. Mum, I can't –

GILL. You'll know who to talk to. You might get us some answers. They certainly don't want to talk to me about –

MICHAEL. They're not going to tell you all the details, Mum. They can't, for security reasons. (*Beat.*) What difference will it make, anyway?

GILL. It'll make a difference to me. I want to know if he'd been put into a dangerous situation that could have been avoided. I want to know if he had the right equipment. I want to know if he was afraid. I want to know 'the details', Michael, because it doesn't make sense and no one wants to answer any of my questions. He was supposed to be there to fix tanks. What was he doing out on a recce, like that?

MICHAEL. He was a soldier. They do what they have to do.

GILL. Don't we all. (*Beat.*) I've been doing a bit of research. I'm not the only one who feels like we're being told half-truths… if not out-and-out lies.

Beat.

MICHAEL. Mum? Me dad's having a hard time. You can see that just by looking at him… he's not himself. He can't seem to do right for doing wrong where you're concerned, can he?

GILL. He could help me get to the bottom of things. That lad at the funeral said our Chris wasn't in an armoured vehicle. His captain said he was. So, who's telling the truth?

MICHAEL. There are all sorts of rumours flying round camp when we suffer losses. Some people like mouthing off, gossiping, filling in gaps. They like gegging in on the drama of it.

GILL. But why won't his commanding officer meet me? Why have the Ministry of Defence refused to answer any of my questions?

MICHAEL. Because you're starting to annoy people, Mum. You're writing letters at the drop of a hat. It's been six months. They've had other losses, other casualties, since our Chris was killed. He wasn't the only one.

GILL. No, but he was my one. They might not think he mattered, but he mattered to me –

MICHAEL. I didn't mean he didn't matter. Jesus. Losing our Chris has torn me apart. There's not a day goes by without –

GILL. Then help me. You could find things out for us, the truth, Michael. It's all I'm asking for.

MICHAEL. You've got to let this go, Mum, really. This isn't good for anyone.

GILL. Isn't it? Do you know what? Some people say that the war in Iraq was illegal, that we shouldn't have even been over there. Clever people, cleverer people than me. I can't understand why that doesn't bother you. If what we did was illegal, then our Chris –

MICHAEL. Jesus Christ! Illegal? What does that mean? You know what I'm bothered about, when I'm out there? Staying alive. I'm bothered about me mates staying alive. That's all that I can afford to be bothered about. What do you think it's like, there? It's not a fucking debating society. We don't sit around whining about the politics of it all.

GILL. Well, maybe you should. (*Beat.*) And I'd prefer it if you didn't use language like that in this house. To me.

MICHAEL. I'm sorry. Can we let this drop once and for all, Mum? Please? Chris is dead. He was a soldier. It's the name of the game and all this isn't gonna bring him back.

MIKE *enters. Beat.*

MIKE. What's going on?

GILL. Ask our Michael.

She leaves but stays at the back of the space, watching her husband and son.

MIKE (*looking at* GILL's *papers*). She's not having it, is she?

MICHAEL. She's gonna have to, because there's nothing she can do about it.

MIKE. It's all she ever wants to talk about. (*Beat.*) I don't know what to do any more. I was hoping you being home would… You know what she's always been like with you and our… She'll listen to you. Maybe you could… spend a bit of time with her… get her out of herself a bit, eh? (*Beat.*) Got to try something, haven't we, mate?

MICHAEL. Yeah. Yeah, we have. (*Beat.*) I need to talk to you, Dad. There's somethin'… somethin' you should know.

MIKE. What is it?

MICHAEL. Sit down.

MIKE *does so.*

One of the lads… who was on patrol with our Chris that night… he's heard somethin'… somethin' nasty.

MIKE. Like what?

MICHAEL. Some… twat… (*Struggling to get it out.*) It'll have been one of them… I can't see any of ours –

MIKE. What is it, Mikie? Just say it.

MICHAEL. Somebody… filmed… our Chris and the others… after they'd… you know… after they'd took the hit.

MIKE. Filmed? What do you mean, 'filmed'? What are you talking about?

MICHAEL. On a phone. The explosion… the aftermath… someone's put it up on the net. Some cunt… It's up there… he's up there… our Chris. (*Beat*.) Our Chris is up there.

GILL *looks at the laptop*.

MIKE. Eh? (*Beat*.) Who would… Why would… (*He looks towards the laptop*.) What sort of a person would film that?

MICHAEL. They're animals, I'm telling you. (*Beat*.) I needed to tell you. In case… I needed to tell you.

MIKE. Jesus. (*Struggling to keep it together*.) You can see… everything, the whole…?

MICHAEL *nods*.

Was he… erm… Were they right… when they said it was… instant, like?

MICHAEL *shakes his head*. MIKE's *breathing hard*.

Jesus. (*Beat*.) He's, err… he's alive? On there?

Beat. MICHAEL *nods*. MIKE *is struggling to breathe*.

Have you –

MICHAEL. No! And neither should you.

MIKE *watches the laptop like it's about to explode*.

Are you listening to me, Dad?

MIKE. Well… I want it off. I want them to take that filth off right now. They can't do –

MICHAEL. It's sorted. I've been onto them. They said they'd look into it. It'll get taken off. Just takes a while.

MIKE. That's not… that can't be right, surely? What kind of a fuckin' world are we –

MICHAEL. I've told you now. In case… I dunno… if it's ever on the news or in the papers or somethin' and… me mum gets to hear about it –

MIKE. Christ, no. (*Beat*.) No. No, that's not gonna happen. No way.

MICHAEL. Didn't wanna have to say anything, but... I'm
sorry, Dad –

MIKE. It's alright, don't worry, don't worry. Er... Yeah, yeah...
Don't you be worrying, son.

MIKE *gives his son a rough pat.* MICHAEL *goes to his
room and starts trying to work out, doing burpees.* CHRIS
appears next to him. He copies his brother. MICHAEL *can
sense that there is something 'wrong'. He stops exercising
and sits on the floor.* CHRIS *stands behind him.* MIKE *pours
himself a drink, then lays newspaper on the floor. He goes to
the laptop and toys with the idea. He can't. He fetches*
CHRIS*'s army boots, boot polish and a cloth. He buffs the
boots like he's washing the stains away. The laptop comes to
life, beckoning.* GILL *struggles not to go to it. Her son is on
there. She is desperate to see him one more time.*

Scene Two

MAYA *steps forward. She reads the names of soldiers followed
by the ringing of a bell.* GILL *sits at a computer.* LUCY *and*
MRS WESTON *face each other.* MIKE *keeps shining the boots.*

MAYA. Sergeant Joseph Johnson, thirty-three.

Bell.

Sapper Luke Allsopp, twenty-four.

Bell.

Staff Sergeant Simon Cullingworth, thirty-six.

Bell.

Flight Lieutenant Dave Williams, thirty-seven.

Bell.

Sergeant Steven Roberts, thirty-three.

Bell.

Lance Corporal Barry Stephen, thirty-one.

Bell.

Captain Andrew Weston, twenty-seven.

Bell.

Private Greg Cope, eighteen.

Bell.

MAYA *leaves as if she has conjured the meeting between* MRS WESTON *and* LUCY. *The sound of News 24 quietly underscores the scene.*

MRS WESTON. I was afraid to come. (*Beat.*) I had to.

LUCY. I knew as soon as the reporter said, 'Just south of Basra.' I felt it. You know, don't you?

MRS WESTON *nods. Beat.*

The day before, a bird had flown into the car when I was coming back from me sister's. Just flew right into it. I had to pull over to clean the windscreen.

Beat.

MRS WESTON. Did you get my letter?

LUCY. I've been meaning to answer… I got so many… from all over… strangers, even.

MRS WESTON. Yes.

LUCY. I haven't had the… I will, though.

Beat.

MRS WESTON. How are you?

LUCY. Going through the motions.

MRS WESTON. Time is a great –

LUCY. Don't. Please.

MRS WESTON. No. No, of course not. Sorry.

Beat.

LUCY. How are you?

MRS WESTON. Going through the motions.

LUCY. When I first wake up in the morning, for a split second –

MRS WESTON. Yes.

LUCY. I hated them at first. The Afghans. The Iraqis. The
women in town with the burkhas on… I'd see an Arab-
looking bloke on a bus and I'd… We all need someone to
blame, don't we? (*Beat*.) Do you hate the people who…?

Beat.

MRS WESTON. I try not to think about it.

LUCY. All them young boys?

MRS WESTON. They're soldiers.

LUCY. So everybody keeps saying. (*Beat*.) Does that make you
feel better?

MRS WESTON. I draw comfort from the fact that he died
doing exactly what he wanted to do.

LUCY. You're lucky then. (*Beat*.) My husband, Graham – we
lie in bed next to each other but we might as well be in different countries. There's a big black hole between us and I
don't know how to get over it. This thing that happened to
our Greg is… Sometimes there's too much…

MIKE *sets the boots down. They are beautiful, shiny and
clean. He leaves.*

MRS WESTON. My voluntary work with families in the regiment helps. (*Beat*.) Are you still involved with –

LUCY. Yes.

MRS WESTON. How do you… Don't you feel any disloyalty
towards the regiment… the men still serving?

LUCY. No.

Beat.

MRS WESTON. It would seem entirely wrong to the memory of my son if –

LUCY. It's too late for my son, Mrs Weston. It's the other sons I have to think about now.

Scene Three

The Kent's house. MIKE *is sat alone.*

GILL. It's late. Are you coming up?

MIKE. Not that tired.

　Beat.

GILL. Me neither. (*Beat.*) I can't get that woman out of my head.

MIKE. What woman?

GILL. The one that was arrested. For reading out the names.

MIKE. Right.

GILL. Don't say it like that.

MIKE. Like what?

GILL. Like that.

MIKE. I didn't mean –

GILL. It was in the paper. It was on the news. (*She picks up a copy of the* Guardian.)

MIKE. Alright. (*Beat.*) Alright.

　GILL *sits next to* MIKE. *Looks through the paper.*

GILL (*reading aloud*). She was 'found guilty of breaching Section 132 of the Serious Organised Crime and Police Act'.

MIKE. I read it, didn't I?

GILL. How can remembering the dead be a serious crime?

MIKE. They're probably making an example of her. Protesting so near to Westminster. They can't have that, can they?

GILL. I don't understand you.

Beat.

MIKE. I can't get into all this now. I've got a banging head.

GILL. That'll be the five or six pints you had in The Railway and the half-bottle of Scotch you polished off when you came in.

MIKE. If things weren't so bloody miserable around here then maybe I wouldn't have to knock it back a bit, eh? (*Beat.*) All this… it's not gonna bring him back, is it? Concerning yourself with all this bloody… nonsense.

GILL. I've tried to explain why I'm concerning myself with all this 'bloody nonsense', as you call it, but you don't understand. In fact, you don't seem to want to understand, so –

MIKE. That's because you've got something in your head and you're not letting go. Bugger anybody else. We don't seem to matter. What we think… doesn't matter.

GILL. I'm trying to… Something good might come out of it.

MIKE. It isn't healthy. Even our Mikie –

GILL. Don't involve our Michael.

MIKE. He is involved. This… woman –

GILL. Maya Johnson –

MIKE. – has got nothing to do with us, with what our Chris –

GILL. What are they afraid of?

MIKE. Listen to yourself! You sound like David bloody Icke. Do you seriously think the government is frightened of what some woman, clearly off her head, is getting up to? We're talking about the actual British government, remember. Stop and think for a minute, Gill. It's ridiculous.

GILL. There's been something not right from the start, Mike. You know it and I know it. Why haven't they had an inquest? Why do they keep fobbing us off, whenever I ask about it? Eh?

MIKE. They have their reasons. There's not just our Chris to consider in all this.

GILL. But they aren't considering him at all, are they?

MIKE. I'm really trying, Gill, honest to God, but if you keep getting into all… What's gonna happen to us, eh? (*Beat.*) What is happening to us? (*Beat.*) Don't you care?

GILL. This isn't about us.

Beat.

MIKE. Will you answer me a question? (*Beat.*) If you carry on with this… how do you think it's gonna affect our Mikie? Hang on, before you say anything, think about it for a minute. Think about it seriously. (*Beat.*) He's a serving soldier for God's sake, Gill. You are bringing into question the very thing he swore to defend to the death. He made an oath. He puts himself on the line for that, every day. Can you imagine how he must –

GILL. Our Michael isn't right. And it's not just because of our Chris. Something's… (*Quietly.*) I know my son, he's not right. My boys were always –

MIKE (*losing it*). For fuck's sake! Our Chris was doing what he wanted to do. He followed in our Michael's footsteps and he was in his bloody element, because he was allowed to be a man for the first time in his life.

GILL. What do you mean by that?

MIKE. You never let 'em be lads. When they were growing up… the things they weren't allowed to do. I watched it happen. I saw them fight and pull against your bloody leash time and time again. As they got older you held on even tighter. So as soon as a chink of light shone through a crack in that door, they couldn't bloody wait to flee.

GILL (*quietly*). I see.

Beat.

MIKE. I shouldn't have said that. I'm sorry. I just want... how you used to be. Not this... We aren't like them people. (*Indicating the article about* MAYA.) We have nothing in common with people like that. (*Beat*.) I'm here. Look at me. Same old, remember? You shouldn't be looking elsewhere at a time like this. It's not right. You shouldn't be thinking about talking to strangers –

GILL *plays with the salt cellar. The war inches closer.*

GILL. – That stranger has been arrested for reading out our son's name. She does that to let people know that, every day, lads like our Chris, young lads with everything to live for, are being killed. And nobody really knows what for.

MIKE. You are relentless. (*Beat*.) It's what I've always loved about you, but if we're not careful it's what's gonna tear us –

GILL. I want to meet her, Mike. (*Beat*.) I am going to meet her.

MIKE. Why? No, really. I want to know exactly. Why?

GILL. Because she knows about the most profound thing that's ever happened to me. And I want to... I need to see what she looks like. I need her to see what I look like. I want to tell her what the boy whose name she has spoken, in public, Christopher Anthony Kent, looked like. I want to tell her that he was real. Not just some name in a newspaper report. I need to, Mike. I just do.

Beat.

MIKE. Okay. But these anti-war... these sites you keep going on... our Michael... he'll think you're being disloyal.

GILL. Our Michael will have to deal with it.

Beat. There is a moment between them.

MIKE. Gill... I didn't mean... I shouldn't have said –

GILL. I know my shortcomings, Mike. I've thought about them a lot, lately. But I've thought about other things, too. (*Beat*.) There is some truth in what you said, I know it, but –

MIKE. I was angry, you say things –

GILL. Let me finish. I spent twenty-odd years trying to protect our kids from all the physical dangers that… You are right. I made them fearful and it's fear that keeps us down.

MIKE. I have never, not for one moment, blamed you for our Chris's –

GILL. This country, this city, what's being done for lads like ours, eh? What do lads round here have going for them? They know how to blag people, how to go on the rob, how to get drunk and fight and how to act big. (*Beat.*) But who's teaching them how to be real men? Ordinary men. Husbands, fathers, good men, like you, who feel useful and valued? No one. No wonder they wanna join the army. (*Beat.*) Nobody seems to care. But somebody should, Mike. That's what I've been thinking about lately. A lot.

MIKE. Sod everybody else, Gill. We've got each other, haven't we? Let's just keep safe. No telly, no radio, no newspapers. Let's leave all this bloody madness to someone else, out there.

GILL (*quietly*). I need to meet Maya Johnson.

A moment between them.

MIKE. Remember our Mikie in all this, please.

GILL. I am. Really, I am.

A moment, then GILL goes and sits at the laptop. LUCY enters and stands. MIKE leaves.

Scene Four

MAYA *steps forward, on the phone.* MRS WESTON *appears at the back of the space. The ghost of her son stands near her. This could be any one of the men, lit only to catch a glimpse – a hand – the back of a head – booted feet – the profile of a soldier, hand raised in salute. Responses in square brackets are not intended to be heard by the audience, but are included here to assist the actor in delivering the speech.*

MAYA. Hello, it's Nanna. Thank you for the lovely card,
sweetheart. ['Mummy didn't help me, I wrote it myself,
Nanna.'] I can see you wrote it yourself. It's fantastic that is.
Is your brother being a good boy? ['He's trying to take the
phone off me. He wants to tell you something important.']
(*Beat. Laughing, fighting back tears*.) Okay then, put him
on. ['Have you got some cake, Nanna?'] Hello, Alex
darling. No. I'm afraid not. You don't get birthday cake at
my age. Is it nice there? ['At the seaside I saw a crab and I
wasn't scared but Ellie said I was.'] You saw a crab? Wow. I
hope it didn't try to nip your toes. ['Love you, Nanna.'] I
love you two. ['I love you three.'] I love you four.
['Mummy says we have to get ready to go to the seaside
now.'] Okay, darling. Don't put the phone down. Put
Hannah back on. Have a lovely time. See you soon, eh?
Bye-bye. (*Beat*.) ['Bye-bye, Nanna.'] Bye-bye, darling.
(*Beat*.) Hello. He was very excited then, wasn't he? ['He
saw a huge crab on the beach yesterday.'] I know. He told
me. ['Mummy said we might live here. We're looking for a
new house.'] (*Beat*.) A new house? You're looking for a new
house there? ['But it's a secret. We can't tell anyone just yet
so don't tell anyone, Nanna.'] I won't. I cross my heart. Can
I… Is your mummy there, darling? ['She's in the bathroom
with Alex, brushing his teeth. Should I go and get her?']
No… no… Don't worry, eh? I'll speak to her another time.
['Mummy says we have to get ready to go now.'] Okay,
sweetheart. Big hugs. Give Alex a hug too. ['Bye Nanna, I
love you.'] I love you too. ['I love you three.'] Four.
['Five.'] Six. ['Seven.'] Eight. ['Nine.'] Ten. ('Have to get
ready now.'] Okay, take care, my love.

The dialling tone. The ghost fades. Both women stand alone.
GILL *logs onto a search engine. Google Earth is projected*
onto film.

Scene Five

MICHAEL *enters, slightly worse for wear.* GILL *immediately gets out of the YouTube site. She switches to the Stop the War Coalition website, and images of the anti-war demonstration in London. Thousands of people marching with placards: 'Not In My Name'.* CHRIS *watches them.*

MICHAEL. You still up?

GILL. Couldn't sleep.

MICHAEL. What are you doing?

GILL. Where was I when all this was happening?

MICHAEL. What?

GILL. There was a peace train… from Liverpool on the fifteenth of February. Just before the war in Iraq.

MICHAEL (*groaning*). And what?

GILL. The amount of people who were in London that day. Ordinary people, from all over. I never realised.

MICHAEL. They wasted their fuckin' time, then, didn't they?

GILL *looks at him.*

It's only a word.

CHRIS *laughs.* MICHAEL *keeps an eye on him, afraid.*

GILL. It's not the word and you know it. It's the way you speak to me. (*Beat.*) What is it? What's going on?

CHRIS *taunts with a couple of lines of Marvin Gaye's 'What's Going On?'*

MICHAEL. Don't know what you're on about.

GILL. Talk to me, Michael.

Following interjections from CHRIS *should underscore and not, in any way, jar the rhythm.*

CHRIS. It's what Sarah couldn't stand about you, isn't it? The way you'd started to talk to her. Foul.

GILL. Michael?

MICHAEL. Why won't you let this thing with our Chris drop? (*Beat.*) It's killing me dad.

GILL. I can't, Michael.

MICHAEL. Might as well align yourself with the fuckin' enemy, then, eh? Our Chris would be made up with that. The murdering – fuckin' – scumbag – Muslim – bastards who blew him to smithereens.

CHRIS (*an American accent*). 'You're either with us or against us.' (*He laughs.*)

GILL. That's not fair and you know it. If people would have answered my questions when our Chris got killed… He was my baby.

CHRIS *imitates a baby crying.*

MICHAEL. What about me? Eh? I'm out there having to deal with shit – day in, day out – and any fucker… and I mean, any fucker… who questions what I'm doing from the comfort of an armchair or a pub stool can go fuck themselves 'cause they haven't got a fuckin' Scooby.

CHRIS. No, but I have –

GILL. I haven't got a 'Scooby', as you call it, about a lot of things, Michael. That's what this is all about. But if I can't get answers that make sense then there's a possibility that he died for nothing. (*Beat.*) I want justice. I need to know the truth.

CHRIS. Go 'ead, Mikie. Put her straight. Go 'ead!

MICHAEL. The only fuckin' justice for our Chris is to make sure them fucking bastards pay. You can't do that. Me dad can't do that. The fucking anti-war movement can't do that. But guess who can? Every fuckin' time I'm on duty, when there's an opportunity. And I'm not ashamed to say it. They're animals. Even their fuckin' women, and kids. Lying, sneaky, murdering, ungrateful little fuckin' rats. (*Beat.*) See,

Mother? I do that so you don't have to worry about 'justice' for our Chris. I do that. For you. (*Beat.*) So you just leave all this other shit. It means nothing. Not out there. Not in the real world.

GILL. What do you mean?

CHRIS. Things that simple, eh, mate?

MICHAEL (*quietly*). I mean, your job is getting him sorted. Get him off the ale. Get him back into work. The taxis even. Anything. Help him claw some fuckin' self-respect back, whatever. Just do what you have to do to get this family back on track, and stop interfering with things you know nothing about.

He goes to leave. CHRIS *stops him. He kisses him on the mouth.*

CHRIS. You doing this out of love, Mikie? Or pain? (*In the voice of the Geordie* Big Brother *presenter.*) 'You decide.'

MICHAEL *is frozen.*

GILL. Michael? Michael? (*Beat.*) Are you alright –

CHRIS. Are you, 'Michael'? Are you alright?

MICHAEL (*looking at* CHRIS). Me? I'm fine.

MICHAEL *leaves.*

Scene Six

MAYA. Sign our petition. Troops out of Iraq now. Bring our boys home.

MIKE *takes the box, the cushion cover and the hookah and puts them in a bin bag. News 24 plays in the background.* MAYA *and* LUCY *are by the Military Family's stall.* MAYA *films* LUCY. GILL *watches from afar.* MICHAEL *is doing scorpion press-ups. His exercise regime is aggressive,*

exaggerated. CHRIS *comes in, watches* MICHAEL *for a bit,
then kicks his arm from under him.* MICHAEL *tries again.*
CHRIS *kicks his arm from under him.* MICHAEL *tries
again,* CHRIS *repeats the action.* MICHAEL *gives up.*
MIKE *takes the bin bag offstage.* MICHAEL *jumps up,
checks himself in the mirror, a grotesque pose of masculinity.*
CHRIS *apes him. A moment between them.* CHRIS *leaves.*

LUCY *talks directly to* MAYA*'s video camera.*

LUCY. Don't be afraid of coming forward. It'll go no further.
And if you come home on leave and can't face going back,
come to us for support. People are behind you. Everyone
knows that things can't be resolved out there through military intervention.

Everyone knows that things are getting worse and worse.

We want to talk to Gordon Brown. We'll go to Downing
Street. We just want the truth. But no one is willing to meet
us. Well, we won't go away. If you want to sign our petition,
please do so, you can do it online. Military Families want
justice for our sons and the sons of this country. We want
you home, immediately.

(*To* MAYA.) How was that? Did I sound okay?

MAYA. Sounded great.

Beat.

LUCY. I didn't notice the red light flashing. Should we do it
again, just in case?

MAYA. If you want to, yeah.

She fiddles around with the video camera.

GILL. Excuse me?

MAYA. Yes, love?

GILL. I wondered if I could have a word.

MAYA. Of course.

GILL. I just… I just wanted to… My son, Christopher, was…
he was killed six months ago in Basra.

MAYA. I'm really sorry.

LUCY. I lost my lad in Iraq too – Greg.

Beat.

GILL. You're Maya Johnson, aren't you?

MAYA *nods*.

LUCY. Lucy Cope.

GILL. Gill Kent. My son was Private Christopher Kent. You read his name out. And you got arrested for it. I wanted to thank you.

LUCY. She's gonna end up locked away if she carries on. She's already had an ASBO, haven't you?

MAYA. I'll keep on until they bring our lads home.

MICHAEL *enters*. CHRIS *watches, from a distance*.

MICHAEL. What's going on here, then?

He glares at GILL.

MAYA. Military Families Against the War. We're campaigning to get the troops out of Iraq and –

MICHAEL. Let's have a look at one of them banners, then. (*He tries to snatch it.*)

LUCY. Hey. Don't touch that.

GILL. I had to come.

MICHAEL. Yeah, me dad said. (*To* MAYA *and* LUCY.) Geeing up for a bit of a party, are you?

MAYA. There's a protest march on at midnight tonight. To the cathedral. It's a peace vigil in aid of –

MICHAEL. Fuckin' soap-dodgers and students giving it loads about shite they know nothin' about. 'Kin 'ell. (*To* GILL.) Behave yourself and go home. (*To* MAYA *and* LUCY.) The lot of youse.

GILL. It's you that needs to go home, you're drunk. (*To* MAYA *and* LUCY.) This is my son, Michael. Sorry.

MICHAEL (*laughing, taking the piss*). 'What do we want? More free money!' More drugs an' ale, that's what we all really need, isn't it, Mum? (*Beat.*) Seriously, it's a waste of fuckin' time, waste of time. 'Wastrels marching in a wasteland just a-wasting time…' / I'm a poet an' don't I fuckin' know it –

LUCY (*to* MAYA). It doesn't rhyme.

GILL. Stop it, Michael.

MICHAEL. Poems don't have to rhyme, love. They've just gotta say something important. Like I just did, then. (*To* MAYA.) About the type of people going on a peace vigil.

LUCY. You haven't got a clue who's going to be on this march. / In fact, you don't seem to have a clue about very much, considering the way you're talking to your mother.

GILL. You're embarrassing us, Michael.

MICHAEL (*to* LUCY). Don't dismiss me like I'm a piece of shit on the bottom of your shoe.

LUCY. Then stop acting like it.

MAYA. I think everyone should just calm down.

GILL (*trying to drag* MICHAEL *away*). We are going home, right now.

MICHAEL (*to* GILL). No, hang on, you seem to think they know what they're talking about so let's have a bit of a debate then, eh? (*To* LUCY, *threatening*.) What makes you think I haven't got a clue, eh?

MAYA. Ignore him, Lucy, he's had a skinful, no use talking to him. (*Beat.*) Can't you see you're upsetting your mum? Go home with her, go on.

MICHAEL. Know what gets me about you fuckin' protestors? You're all liars –

GILL. That's enough, Michael.

MICHAEL. – Just a good day out for you, isn't it? Get your butties sorted for the coach, a few scoops to get you in the mood, eh? –

LUCY. Is that right?

MICHAEL. – All together with your little chants and your little slogans… I was on leave when Condoleezza Rice was in Liverpool, you were all out in force then, weren't ya? Some stupid cunt –

GILL. Michael, stop it.

MICHAEL. – with a scarf covering her head's on a megaphone, chanting, 'We all live in a terrorist regime.' Seriously. That's what she was getting youse all chanting. I wanted to punch her cheeky fuckin' lights out –

MAYA. Everything's solved by violence, is it?

MICHAEL. – You can't go on marches, chanting stuff like that, in an actual terrorist regime, you daft bunch of bastards. Be honest. It wouldn't be allowed, love –

LUCY. Why don't you go home and sober up?

MICHAEL. – You just wanna feel good about yourselves, don't you? Close to the barricades. Couple of fireworks now and again and a bit of a run-in with the bizzies –

GILL (*tugging at him, trying to pull him away*). Come away, Michael –

MICHAEL. – just to remind you that you're doing something important, something 'dangerous'. Then the adrenalin starts kicking in, doesn't it, eh? Bit of a buzz. Bit of danger for a couple of hours, in the sun, then off you go. Shit. That feels like living, doesn't it, eh? –

MAYA. You don't know what you're talking about, son.

MICHAEL. – Better than Alton fuckin' Towers that. 'I make a difference. I put myself on the line for what I believe in.' Do you fuck –

GILL (*crying*). Shut it, Michael, just shut it –

MICHAEL. – Liars. I'll give you a better idea of putting yourself on the line. Hang around the taxi rank at the bottom end of town on a Friday night and see what that feels like. Or go

to the match of a Saturday when there's a big game on an'
the promise of a big fuck-off ruck –

LUCY. Is that right, yeah?

MICHAEL. – These sensitive little boys you're marching on
behalf of? You wanna see them when they're out on a raid.
The adrenalin pumping, kicking down doors, getting in there.
I mean, right in there. Anybody mouth off or complain, old,
young or indifferent… fuck them – (*He mimes smashing
someone in the face with a rifle, with sound effects.*)

GILL. Stop it stop it stop it –

MICHAEL. – The family fuckin' dog barks out of turn? Shoot
the little fucker. (*He mimes blowing a dog away, with
sound effects. To an imaginary mother.*) 'Shut that fuckin'
kid up now!'

He kicks over the stall and starts ripping down the banners.

GILL (*belting him*). That's enough.

MICHAEL *stops.*

MICHAEL (*to* GILL). You want the truth? People like it. They
want it. It's in us. In all of us –

LUCY. Maya? I'm phoning the police –

GILL. Please don't. Don't. He's not himself. I'll get him home.
Michael! Get home, now –

MICHAEL. Know what offends me about you lot? You pretend
like you're actually making a difference. What a lie. Us soldiers, we're not liars. We're really fuckin' honest to our-
selves. We have to be. 'Cause we know what it's really
about. Following orders. (*Beat.*) I'm telling you. We live it
every day. It's in every single one of us.

GILL *breaks down,* MAYA *holds her.* MICHAEL *exits.*

GILL. He wasn't brought up to behave like that. I swear. He's
always been a good boy. He'd never spoken to me like that
before in his life. Never.

LUCY*'s mobile beeps a text message.*

MAYA. Ssshhh. It doesn't matter. It's all right. There's no real harm. He was drunk. He's lost his brother, there's bound to be some –

LUCY (*reading the text*). I'm sorry, love, but… Maya?… Kadife from the SWP said they want us to move to County Terrace. It's a better spot, there, apparently. For the press and that, later.

GILL. I didn't expect… I feel terrible. I'm sorry.

MAYA. Don't worry about it. (*Beat.*) Here… take a leaflet. It's got all our details on. Have a look at the website. Got all sorts of things coming up. Campaigns, marches. That sort of thing. Come along if you want to.

GILL. Oh no… I just… I just wanted to meet you. And say thanks. I've never been one for –

MAYA. None of us have, love.

LUCY. Maya? It's time to move on.

The women start to pack up. GILL *leaves in the opposite direction.* MRS WESTON *steps forward.*

Scene Seven

The WESTONS *get ready to go out for the evening to a regimental dinner. Everything is stiff, formal.* COLONEL WESTON *has a chest full of medals.*

COLONEL WESTON. I'm rather looking forward to this evening, aren't you? (*Beat.*) Olivia?

MRS WESTON. Sorry, darling, what was that?

COLONEL WESTON. Are you alright?

MRS WESTON. Yes, yes of course. (*Beat.*) What did you say?

COLONEL WESTON. I said I'm really looking forward to this evening. And then I asked you if you were, too.

MRS WESTON. Yes, I am.

MICHAEL starts to undress. When MRS WESTON *is ready, she sits still, watching her husband put the finishing touches to his uniform.* MAYA *and* LUCY *bring boxes of files and a laptop on.*

LUCY. So they said we can set the peace camp up outside the town hall, now? No backtracking.

MAYA. After all the publicity we've had, the council wouldn't dare.

LUCY. They reckon we've had offers of all sorts – (*She checks her mobile.*) tents, camping equipment, gas cylinders and a couple of them camping stoves. Cup of tea first thing in the morning… What more could you ask for?

MAYA. They're alright, them little stoves, you know, we'll be able to have a hot meal.

LUCY. Kadife says the local takeaways will sort us out. There's loads of curry houses and that round that way.

LUCY's mobile rings.

(*On the phone.*) Hello? Hi Jan. (*Beat.*) It's a no, I'm afraid. We don't want the lads to think we're jumping on every bandwagon going. (*Beat.*) It could affect morale. (*Beat.*) Speak to you later.

MAYA. The anti-nuclear demo at the airbase?

LUCY. She sort of knew we wouldn't agree to it. She was fine about it, like. Wanted to know if there was any point in coming to a meeting to try and persuade us.

MAYA. She's a nice enough woman, but when they get their teeth into something, these political types. They don't want to let go, do they?

Beat. They laugh.

Right. Let's have a go at this press release.

Beat. They go to the laptop. LUCY *logs on. They set to work. Beat.*

MRS WESTON. Whenever I think of him, I try to think of his face on the day he was accepted into Sandhurst. (*Beat.*) He was happy that day, wasn't he? (*Beat.*) I didn't imagine it, did I?

COLONEL WESTON. No, darling, you didn't imagine it.

MRS WESTON. No... Right. Shall we go?

He offers her his arm. They leave.

Scene Eight

MICHAEL *is alone. He kneels in front of a bucket of water.*
GILL *enters, not seeing him at first.*

GILL. Michael? Michael? (*She checks around for him.*) Are you here? (*Beat.*) Answer me? Michael.

She sees him. MICHAEL *is staring at the bucket.*

Michael? Are you alright?

MICHAEL. It's mad, isn't it?

GILL. You should be ashamed of yourself. Making a show –

MICHAEL. I'm not a good man, Mum. I'm not –

GILL. Stop being so pathetic. You must have been drinking all day, no wonder you feel bad –

MICHAEL. No, no... I'm talking about everything –

GILL. What? –

MICHAEL. The lies, the pretence.

GILL. Stop feeling sorry for yourself –

MICHAEL. I deserve to be punished. I do –

GILL. You should go back and apologise when you've sobered up. I've never been so ashamed in my life.

MICHAEL (*shouting*). I'm not talking about getting pissed up and kicking off. (*Beat. Quietly.*) That was nothing. I mean… I deserve to be punished for something bad.

GILL. What are you talking about?

MICHAEL. I never… never spoke to our Chris before he was killed. I told you I was gonna take care of him. I had no intention… Wouldn't even let myself think about him. I'm like that, see, a bastard.

GILL. Stop it. That's not important now, come on, get yourself up.

She tries to help him up, he resists.

MICHAEL. There are other things. Worse things –

The bloodied ghost of CHRIS *appears.* MICHAEL *starts to cry.*

CHRIS. You big pussy. Stop snivelling, soldier.

MICHAEL. Chris. Oh Chris, you don't know, lad.

GILL. What are you on about? What's wrong, Michael?

MICHAEL. You don't know what you made me do.

GILL. Michael, stop it. Our Chris is… It's okay. It's okay. (*Shouting.*) Mike?

She tries to get MICHAEL *to stand. He resists.*

CHRIS. Don't be putting that shit on me, Mikie. You've gone, mate. There's no coming back from where you are now. Do yourself a favour and pull the plug. You're giving good soldiers a bad name, aren't ya?

MICHAEL. Don't look at me like that. (*Beat.*) Hurt me if it'll make you feel better.

He grabs GILL*'s hand and starts to hit himself with it. She struggles.* CHRIS *laughs.*

Come on, hurt me.

He plunges his head in the bucket of water. GILL *struggles to pull him out.* MICHAEL *stays under.* GILL *panics.*

CHRIS. Who the fuckin' hell ever drowned themselves in a bucket of water, ya ted?

GILL (*pulling him up*). Stop it, Michael, stop it.

He does so. GILL *soothes him.*

Oh sweetheart, my baby, don't, don't, it's alright, I'm here. What are you doing? What is it, love? Talk to me.

CHRIS. Are you gonna tell her? Have you got the guts to spill your guts? Eh, soldier?

MICHAEL. I have to tell you something, Mum, but there'll be no going back for us.

GILL. You're not making sense, Michael –

CHRIS. Go on, my son. Spit it out. Tell her about the sprog. (*He mimes slitting his throat.*)

MICHAEL. You can't look at me when I say it… you can't.

CHRIS. But you made her look, didn't ya, that young Iraqi girl? So you could see the look in her eyes, eh? How exciting was that? (*Beat.*) I'm here to return the favour, Mikie.

MICHAEL. Don't. Please don't.

GILL. Michael, you're scaring me now. What's wrong?

MICHAEL (*whispering*). The last time I was on leave, before our Chris got killed?

CHRIS. Go on. Leave her with something to believe in. Tell her the truth, that's what she's always asking for, isn't it?

Beat.

GILL. Yes?

MICHAEL. Savages… you called them Yanks savages. The lads who –

GILL. What are you on about, Michael?

MICHAEL *cries, struggles to get it out. Through the following speech,* GILL *interjects, calling his name.*

CHRIS. 'Moral decisions', remember? That sprog tried to make a moral decision, didn't he? He dared to stand up to that sergeant, he refused to fuck that young girl. Took some guts that, didn't it, eh? Now, he was a soldier. Not like you. The towel-heads weren't happy about you defiling their women, though, were they? When they put up a fight, that poor sprog kopped for it because you fucked off and left him there, on his own. (*He mimes slitting his own throat.*) 'If you're not with us… you're against us.' Could have been me, that.

MICHAEL. No… no…

GILL. 'No' what, Michael?

MICHAEL. I don't know what I'm doing any more –

GILL. What have you done? Who are you talking to, Michael?

MICHAEL. £1300. I took £1300 for our Chris –

CHRIS. Better than *Deal Or No* fuckin' *Deal*, isn't it?

GILL. You're scaring me, Michael, try and stand up.

MICHAEL. I wanted to hurt somebody for what they did to you, / I swear.

CHRIS. You like it too much, Mikie, to blame it on a one-off.

MICHAEL. You have to believe me, Mum… it was different before.

GILL. For God's sake, love, what is it? –

CHRIS. I looked up to you. You're a fucking joke, lad, aren't you? Tell her. Be a man –

GILL (*shouting*). Mike? Mike?

CHRIS *comes very close to* MICHAEL.

CHRIS. When I was that high, (*Indicates the height of a small child.*) I looked out the gates at you playing footie with your mates. I watched the way you walked and talked. I studied every fuckin' move you made. Know why, Mikie? 'Cause I wanted to be you. I loved you so fuckin' much, I wanted to be you.

MICHAEL. I didn't mean… I swear. Chris? Chris?

GILL. It's alright, love, I'm going to phone the doctor, okay? I'll be two minutes.

MICHAEL *grabs his mum.*

MICHAEL. No. No. Don't leave me. Just listen to me.

He tries to get it together. The moment of courage?

CHRIS (*willing* MICHAEL *to say it*). Now's your chance to confess. Go on. Born as new. That's what they say, innit? Grab that little bit of soul back, Michael.

He offers his hand. MICHAEL *tries but can't touch him.*

I'm throwing you a fuckin' lifeline here, mate. (*He screams.*) Take it, you stupid cunt, I love you. Take it. (*Thrusting his hand at* MICHAEL.) Tell her what you've done and give us all a chance to be born as new.

GILL (*terrified*). What is it you want to tell me, sweetheart? What is it you want to say?

We hear the front door open. It's the explosion that killed CHRIS. *Silence.* MICHAEL *takes a moment before pulling back.*

MICHAEL. Nothing.

Beat. He dips his head in the bucket and gets it together.

Nothing. I just… I lost it. Sorry. I'm alright. (*Beat.*) I swear. I'm alright. (*Beat.*) Shut the door on your way out. I want to get changed. I'm going back tonight.

GILL. You can't go back in this state.

MICHAEL. It's being here that's doing my head in.

Beat.

GILL. You're not due back till tomorrow, you can't… Where will you –

MICHAEL. I'll crash at Snowy's.

GILL. Wait till the morning… please… see the doctor… You're not yourself, Michael.

MICHAEL. I'm who I need to be.

GILL. What is it you need to tell me? (*Beat.*) There's nothing you could –

MICHAEL. I'm a good soldier, Mum. A fucking good soldier. (*Beat.*) I can't wait to get back. So I can carry on being a fucking good soldier. (*Beat.*) Shut the door on your way out.

There is a moment between them. MICHAEL *puts on a front.* GILL *leaves.* MICHAEL *exercises, full of power.* MIKE *and* GILL *face each other.*

MIKE. What's up? What's going on?

GILL. Jesus Christ.

MIKE. What? What is it?

GILL. I… I don't know… I… I don't know.

MIKE. Is it our Michael?

GILL. He's going back tonight.

MIKE. Tonight? He's only due back tomorrow, isn't he? Is there something up? What's wrong, love? (*Beat.*) Tell me. Is there something wrong with our Mikie?

GILL. No, no, he's alright. He's just… going to stay with a friend. (*Beat.*) It's what he wants.

A moment of desolation between them. MIKE *leaves. He pours a drink and sits in the dark, away from his wife and son.* GILL *goes to her own space. The laptop beckons. The sound of war, terrifying, ugly, starts to invade her head. Images of boots, marching, running, kicking, come up on the screens. She goes to the laptop, hovers. The sound of war increases. She struggles not to succumb to the laptop.* MICHAEL *keeps exercising, he grunts harder as he works.* MIKE *starts to cry. He sobs.* GILL *can hear them both. She steels herself, sits and types. The YouTube logo comes up on one screen. Then another. Then another. She types in: 'British soldiers get ambushed in Afghanistan.' The screens show various grainy YouTube video stills, just waiting to be clicked open. She clicks on one. Takes a breath, watches. It's the lead-up to the ambush and murder of her son.* MRS WESTON *steps forward with her son's last letter and reads.*

MRS WESTON. Here, where life and death walk hand in hand, I feel a huge sense of belonging. To the terrain, the rhythm of this life and especially to the guys. I am more myself here than I have ever been. I feel a little guilty for this. In relation to you especially, Mum. I know you often worried about me, my distance, my quietness. I think maybe you took it as a slight? That there was something wrong between us? I'm sorry for that. If you could see me here you'd see a different me. I am at ease with myself. (*Beat. She continues.*) Yesterday I went for a walk in the hills, to watch the sun go down (sunsets are quite remarkable here). I saw a man, an enemy, doing the same thing. We both had weapons, cocked and ready. I thought the end had come. Oddly, I wasn't afraid. We stood looking at each other for about twenty, thirty seconds or so, when the sun dropped between two valleys, casting the most beautiful red-orange glow over us. It was impossible not to look at it. I felt it and he felt it too. I never once thought he would shoot me and I never once thought of shooting him. I felt safer than I have ever felt before. (*She reads the rest of the letter to herself until the salutation.*) God bless you and may Allah, peace be upon Him, send His blessing, also.

GILL *weeps and caresses the screen. Blackout.*

Scene Nine

MAYA *and* LUCY *at the peace camp.* MICHAEL *enters with a suitcase. He puts it down and stands to attention.* CHRIS *enters and stands at ease, facing his brother.*

MAYA (*through a megaphone*). Please bring the biggest photograph you've got of your loved one who was killed. Let's show those in positions of power what our sons and daughters actually look like. Let's line the streets with them. Be proud of who they were, not of how they died.

At the opposite side of the space, MRS WESTON *hangs a framed photograph of her son, on duty in a desolate desert,*

next to one of her husband, at an officers' mess dinner.
MIKE *and* GILL *face each other across the divide.*

MIKE. I don't want you to go.

GILL. I have to.

MICHAEL. You do what you have to do, to survive.

MIKE. This isn't like you. You would never have –

GILL. It's who I am now.

MICHAEL. There are things, in here (*His head.*) that you have to keep in check. Gotta stay strong.

MIKE. I need you home. With me –

GILL. Don't.

MICHAEL. It's me or you. End of.

MIKE. Why are you doing this?

GILL. I have to.

MICHAEL. Don't trust any fucker, you get me? Don't believe a word they say. Self-preservation, isn't it?

MIKE. What about me?

GILL. Come with me.

MICHAEL. Any weakness… anything at all… people can smell it.

MIKE. All those people, that pain? (*Beat.*) I haven't the heart for it.

GILL. It's the only thing I have the heart for, now.

MICHAEL. I'm at the heart of fuckin' power. I smell of fuckin' power, man. I fuckin' rock at what I do. Nobody fucks with me. 'Cause I don't give a fuck about anything or anyone. (*He moves towards his dad.*)

MIKE. What about our Mikie?

GILL. That's not our Michael.

MIKE. Don't say that.

MICHAEL. See you, Dad.

They embrace.

You look after yourself, mate.

MIKE. Be careful, lad. Watch your back, know what I mean?

MICHAEL. Don't you worry. I'm good at that. Very good at it.

They shake hands, then an awkward, rough hug.

(*To* GILL.) Ta-ra then, Mum.

He kisses her. It's formal, lacking in warmth from either of them.

GILL. I love you, Michael. (*Beat.*) You know that, don't you?

MICHAEL. Love you too, Mum. (*Beat.*) See you. Take care.

He goes to leave.

GILL. Mikie?

He stops. It's the first time she's ever called him that.

I'm really sorry.

MICHAEL. For what?

GILL. Should never have let you and our Chris go.

MICHAEL. Best thing you ever did for me. (*Beat.*) Our Chris
was unlucky. Wasn't cut out for the life. Whereas, me…
Don't be worrying. I'll be alright. I promise.

He leaves.

MIKE. I'm terrified he won't come back.

GILL. I'm terrified he will.

Scene Ten

GILL *joins the other* MOTHERS. *They put Military Family T-shirts on, spread leaflets and banners around the space. Putting photographs of their sons around the space. Photographs of other mothers' sons. The* FATHERS *and* SONS *stand to attention at the back of the space.* MRS WESTON *folds the letter.* GILL *talks to* MAYA *and* LUCY.

LUCY. It's a bit sensitive this, like, but… because most of the food has been donated from the Muslim community, the takeaways, an' that… and we've had loads of support from them women as well, so… Well, Kadife wants to know if we'd wear headscarves when we speak, you know, as an act of solidarity?

MAYA. Piss off. I've just had me hair done. (*Beat.*) I'm not being funny, each to their own, but… No. Definitely not.

GILL *shakes her head.*

LUCY. I wasn't too happy about it myself, but I said I'd mention it. (*Beat.*) Are you ready, Gill?

GILL *nods and steps up to the podium.*

GILL. I'm shaking like a leaf, so you'll have to forgive me if I get a bit mixed-up. I've never spoken in front of people before and I don't know anything about politics, so I can only talk about me and my family. About how this… this war has affected us. (*Beat.*) My son, Christopher, was killed in action in Basra. He was nearly twenty. (*Beat.*) There's nothing like losing your child. Nothing. If me or my husband could have changed places with our Chris, we would have. He'd hardly had time to be a man. I still see him walking through the door in his school uniform, acting the goat, with his brother, on the way to school… (*Beat.*) Although we are still here, walking around, talking, and behaving like we're still alive… we might as well have been blown apart with him. Because there's nothing of my family left any more. This thing, this terrible thing that happened to us… has changed us beyond recognition. We'll never be the same again. I started off saying I could only talk about my family, but looking round... I see me everywhere. In you. And you. All of us here... hoping for the well-being of our kids. There's nothing between us... we're the same... our lads were the same... I see that when I speak about me and mine up here, I'm speaking about us all. (*Beat. She finds strength.*) He never knew what he wanted, our Chris. (*Beat.*) Never found his place or his rhythm. I know there are a lot of lads like him. (*Beat.*) Me eldest lad is still serving so I don't want to say his name. He's done two tours of Iraq. I fear for him. Here or there, I fear for him. (*Beat.*) He's not the same lad any more. We used to be really close, but... That's what this war has done to us. I feel like I've lost two sons. (*Beat.*) He doesn't agree with me doing this. (*Beat.*) I'll be honest, standing up here, on a protest march, camping out... feels like something somebody else should be doing, not me. (*Beat.*) But I can't let them get away with... I have to do something. (*Beat.*) I've written to Tony Blair... asking him to meet with me. I want to look him in the eyes and ask him why his wife was driving round London in a £50,000 armoured car, paid for by us, when soldiers were being blown to pieces driving fiberglass jeeps in Iraq. I want to ask him a lot of things. (*Beat.*) I'm not the first mother he's refused to meet. He's never met any of the families of the soldiers killed. He refused when he was Prime Minister and he refuses now. (*Beat.*) He once said that history would be his judge. Then he should be willing to put himself up to be judged, shouldn't he? Because they've made things ten times worse in Iraq. (*Beat.*) Now it's Afghanistan's turn to go the same way. Well, someone has to say no. Someone has to say, 'Send your lads to be maimed or killed. I want to keep mine safe.' It has to be people like us. (*Beat.*) These women have been trying to get justice for a long time. They refuse to go away. And I'm glad of them. (*Beat.*) Our Chris is just another statistic. But he was my son. My lovely, lively son. An ordinary lad, who liked the odd pint, went to the match when he could afford to, and was into his music. There's a lot out there, just like him. And they matter. To us.

As the lights go down, MAYA *reads out the names of the last soldiers.*

MAYA. Territorial Army Personal, Sergeant Peter Mahoney, forty-four.

Bell.

Sergeant Chris Hickey, thirty.

Bell.

Lance Corporal Shaun Brierley, twenty-eight.

Bell.

Lance Corporal Thomas Richard Keyes, twenty.

Bell.

Fusilier Gordon Gentle, nineteen.

Bell.

As MAYA *fades out, video of the real Military Families Against the War shows on the screen.*

The End.

A Nick Hern Book

Ten Tiny Toes first published in Great Britain as a paperback original in 2008 by Nick Hern Books Limited, 14 Larden Road, London W3 7ST, in association with Liverpool Everyman and Playhouse

Ten Tiny Toes copyright © 2008 Esther Wilson

Esther Wilson has asserted her right to be identified as the author of this work

Cover image: Uniform
Cover design: Ned Hoste, 2H

Typeset by Nick Hern Books, London
Printed and bound in Great Britain by CPI Antony Rowe, Chippenham, Wiltshire

A CIP catalogue record for this book is available from the British Library

ISBN 978 1 85459 528 7